Six Million Trees

Hi Hannah
 Here is a book
I wrote
 about tree planting.
Cheers eh

Six Million Trees

Kristel Derkowski

Rock's Mills Press
Oakville, Ontario

Published by
ROCK'S MILLS PRESS

For information, contact
customer.service@rocksmillspress.com.
Library and Archives Canada Cataloguing in Publication data is available
from the publisher.

Cover design: Kristel Derkowski and Dylan Johnston

www.rocksmillspress.com

Six Million Trees

0

The only thing we do is plant trees. That's what makes people crazy.

It's the only thing we do. We plant trees all day, one at a time, over and over and over again. Every day, all day, we plant trees.

We're trying to make money — to make good money — so we plant them quickly. We have to plant fast, fast and non-stop, ten hours a day. Ten hours a day, ten cents a tree —

To make two, three, four hundred dollars a day —

How many trees do you have to plant to make that kind of money when you're being paid ten cents per tree?

How many trees can a person possibly plant?

It's the only thing we do.

By the end of it, people go crazy. Bush crazy, we call it. Because we've been living in the bush for a long time. Because we haven't seen anyone else. We haven't done anything else. We plant trees all day. It's the only thing we do.

1

This season was 71 days, and it wasn't supposed to be that long, but then a lot of things went wrong.

Day 71, the final night, the guys were whipping each other with leather belts. Each of them smoking a cigarette with one hand and whipping a belt with the other, trying to leave belt-welts on each other, on top of everything else. It was pouring rain outside, hammering rain on the roof of my tent, almost deafening. I was trying very hard to stay awake and my eyes were open but I couldn't see anything because it was perfectly black out, sticky black like tar between the raining clouds and the flooding gravel pit. So when I walked to the mess tent I walked right through the growing ponds on the gravel, walked ankle-deep through the black creeks of rainwater, and I just kept walking, splashing through because by then it didn't matter either way. It took me three hours to crawl out of my tent and into the rain, three hours of eyes-glued-open against the blackness while my face was all fiery with some kind of fever and I was curled into a fetal position and shivering and mostly just thinking that I wanted to stand up and move—

I kept hearing the pounding stereo beats and all the drunk people yelling, cheering, yelling while they whipped each other—and the deafening rain-beats and sometimes low rolling thunder—and I kept listening to all of this and wanting to go towards it.

Eventually I did. I crawled out of my tent and put a can of beer in my coat pocket, lukewarm beer beaded with raindrops, and I splashed into the mess tent. I smoked a cigarette with Stefan and then my vision went black around the edges so I slunk away, carefully into a chair and I drank beer to make my head stop spinning.

It didn't really work but that didn't really matter either. I stayed there, shoulders slumped against the plastic chair and everything damp under a winter coat and two sweaters, and still shivering on the inside. That was when Yukon came over to tell me about the glory of the day—

Today was fucking glorious, he told me, and I agreed, Of course it was fucking glorious.

He asked me where I'd been all night and I told him:
I'm dying.
And he said, I'm really sorry to hear that.
I said, Me too, and then I asked him to bring me to the hospital again tomorrow, so he did. Meanwhile in the low yellowy light in front of us Mandog was trying to dodge a whip from a belt and he slipped in some puddle of beer or rain on the floor. He went crashing down and his flailing belt snatched the speaker off a plastic table, so a thousand beer cans went clattering down with him and everyone was cheering and pounding on whatever tables were still standing. By the end of the night, none of the tables were still standing because the tree planters were throwing each other against the plastic furniture and against the walls of the mess

tent until everything was broken, and all the tables snapped in half and all the chairs cracked up around the armrests, and beer cans and plates and clothing and garbage covering the ground. And by then the pitch-blackness had crawled across all my vision and I was unconscious, curled in a fever on top of my damp sleeping bag, still wearing two sweaters and a damp winter coat, but at least I'd changed my socks so they weren't soaked through anymore. The rain was still pounding on top of all the tents, and the rain was making ponds and creeks in the blind blackness of the gravel pit until the dawn broke.

At dawn everyone woke up again drunk and staggering, went splashing around in the puddles of rainwater and vomit—though the vomit had gone trickling into the wet gravel so the only thing left of it was little splatters of yellow corn—and we staggered around giggling at that. We ripped all the tents down, and threw the broken furniture in the garbage trailer along with everything else: along with all the food, the blankets, broken shovels, broken boots, broken tents, and the fifty thousand plastic bags that had held six million trees before we planted them.

In the high noon daylight Yukon and I drove the garbage trailer to the dump and threw all the white plastic furniture and white plastic bags and white plastic bread out on the ground so someone could run over it with a bulldozer while the seagulls made white circles in the sky overhead. Then Yukon dropped me at the hospital and we all parted ways. Then the bush camp was gone, dissolved, and the trees were all planted, and that was the end of all that.

And at the end of all that, it took me a long time to figure out what to do with myself. Turns out, I wasn't even dying.

2

Our season, this year, began and ended in the rain. In the beginning it was early-May rains: drizzling sleet freezing everything into steely shades of grey. The churned-up roadsides were blackish mud and whitish frosting; the distant treeline was dark-grey, shadow-grey behind the mist. And everything between—stumps, sticks, snow, swamp—massive untamed landscapes all in shades of cold indifferent grey.

For the first few days our hands froze into claws. The seedlings themselves were frozen, too; they came frozen in clumps straight from the tree nursery. We would kneel at the caches on the roadside, crouch beside the tarps where the bundles of baby trees were all piled in their white-plastic bags. We'd rip the bags open with frozen hands shaped like bloody hooks, and we'd grind our white-hard fingertips into the cracks between the root-pods to sever them apart. We'd shove trees by frozen handfuls into the plasticky bowels of our tree-planting bags. Shrug into the wet shoulder straps, clip the heavy waistband closed, tight, and charge back into the land. Heads down, half-closed eyes gazing groundward, with sleet tapping our hard hats and sleet seeping into our shirts and into our pants and socks and underwear.

One tree at a time:

Kick at the ground, stab it with the shovel, open a hole with a twist of the arm;

Slide the root-pod of a tree into the little opening there, and stomp the hole closed with one boot;

Then two steps, forward;

And again,

And again.

The trees were baby spruce or baby pine. Their stems were just the length of a finger or the length of two hands, or anywhere between. Their roots were held in cylindrical pods of dirt, wrapped in cheesecloth, sized to fit roughly in a fist.

Once every six seconds—or so—we would each bury one little pod in the soil, with one little stem standing up and sticking straight out.

And then another.

We would carry about three hundred trees at a time, piled into our planting bags, strapped to our shoulders and waists. The bags hung off our hips, one on either side. One bundle of seedlings inside each planting bag; a hundred-fifty-odd trees hanging from either hip. We'd take one tree out at a time, and plant it in the ground. And then another, and more-or-less three hundred more. Then march back to the roadside cache, and kneel, and claw, and refill and charge in—

Faster this time. More trees, more money.

More trees, more money: that's it, that's how it goes.

Our hands would be frozen while everything else was burning: back muscles, thighs, shoulders and arms—knees, elbows burning as they creaked—everything rusty from the off-season—eyes and cheeks burning under the cold white sun—bloody knuckles and blistering palms, frozen numb and still burning.

Eyes down, head down, spine horizontal and one hand in the ground. The other hand clamped onto an undersized shovel: shovel less than the length of an arm, slicing the earth open, twisting and swinging away to slice somewhere else—and again—once every six seconds, or so—

Faster. More trees, more money. Three hundred trees in the land, then back to the road. One tree every six seconds—

Faster. Back at the roadside, knees in the mud, we would chug water out of gas cans, water almost-frozen like everything else. Once in a while, we'd pause to inhale a sandwich or a piece of fruit or some sugar-packed power-snack, gripping and ripping with those bare blackstained claws.

And charge in again, bent-backed. Faster. More trees, more money. Simple enough.

Around 6 pm each day, we'd empty our bags for the last time, clip them light around the waist. We would pick up the almost-frozen gas jerries, shrug into our muddy backpacks. Carry our shovels, lower our heads and stomp or sway or stagger back towards the van.

Fifteen people in the van, and our gear on the roof. The windows would go white and the swampy wetness of the clearcuts would seep out of our socks, boots, seep out of our pants into the fuzzy grey carpet. Shoulder-to-shoulder, we would share food, words, sweat and foggy breath, and Konrad would drive us back to camp.

That was the beginning of it. That's how the days went by.

More money, more trees. Simple enough.

3

The weather changed on Day 12. There was sun, that day, instead of mist and sleet.

5:48 in the morning, with the dawn just barely broken, all of the telltale signs were there. A dead-frozen night usurped by overbright daylight and noisy birds: evidently it was going to be a hot May day in Northern Ontario.

I woke up wrapped in a fleece blanket inside of a sleeping bag inside of another sleeping bag underneath a duvet, wearing two pairs of pants, two cotton socks under two thermal socks, and two shirts under two sweaters with two hoods both pulled up.

I woke up with my nose frozen by the subzero nighttime and the rest of me far too comfortable, tantalizingly warm and limply horizontal on the ground, and I woke up with my tongue stuck to the roof of my mouth from dehydration.

At 5:48 my watch was beeping from the floor beside my head. I reached one hand out into the frigid air, shut off the alarm. Reluctantly, draggingly, I pulled myself half-upright and pulled off those warm-dry layers of sleeping clothes, pulled on some damp-dirty layers for the workday ahead.

The walls of the tent around me were soaked in condensation and they were glowing with the extra-white sun. The birdsong was louder than the roar of the generator. For the first time that season, I left my heavy winter coat in my tent. I unzipped the door and crawled out into the sprawling quarry where we'd camped. Pocketed my hands, tucked my chin into my jacket, dragged my feet across the gravel towards the mess tent.

Tom told us that it would be hot, that morning. That's how he started the meeting. It was part of Company policy that he had to talk about safety every morning, in some form or another, so Tom told us to consider wearing sunscreen that day.

He told us that he'd never worn sunscreen when he was a tree planter, and that one day he'd woken up with bubbles growing behind his ear. He'd gone to the clinic and a doctor had told him he had skin cancer, to which he'd responded,

Well, fuck.

Tom was very casual. Every morning, he opened the meeting by saying:

Alright, guys.

And everyone would go quiet.

Alright, guys — with one hand in the pocket of his jeans and the other holding an energy drink. Shoulder-length hair, scruff on the face. Slow words with the vowels extra-long, drawn-out and rounded.

Tom didn't actually have skin cancer, as it turned out. It had been a slight misdiagnosis. But he told us, now, that he was at a very high risk of skin cancer, because he'd never worn sunscreen when he was a tree planter, and because he'd been living in the bush all summer, day-in-day-out under the sun, for more than nine years now.

He told us: When I was a planter I just thought, Fuck it, and I never bothered—But as it turns out, sunscreen might not be a bad idea, on days like this—Actually, it might even be a good idea, if you don't want to have cancer.

And I thought about that, briefly. And then I thought, Well, Fuck it.

The second point he addressed that morning was the issue of mold on the trees.

Don't plant trees that are already dead, said Tom.

And we kind of laughed about that, although it was serious—the same way we kind of laughed about skin cancer, and about pretty much everything else.

The tree nursery was sending us seedlings that were already dead. There was parasitic mold growing in the bundles of jack pine, and the trees were dying before we had a chance to plant them. Tom told us that we should be sorting through each bundle, and pulling out the moldy trees and leaving them out on the roadside. The Client wanted to see all the dead seedlings, wanted to see how many trees were being wasted. The Client didn't want to pay us to fill their land with trees that were already dead.

We listened, and we smiled, and we stood, sat, stretched. We sipped on coffee and cigarettes, we laced our boots, we wrapped our fingers in duct tape. When the meeting was over, we shouldered our packs and shuffled into the vehicles.

Two crews drove in vans, and two crews drove in reappropriated school buses. Four crews of fifteen-ish each, off to the cut blocks and spread out to work. Sixty planters, or so—spread across the clearcuts to plant one tree and then another tree and then another. And so on.

4

I was working next to Ben that day. Konrad tossed us out of the van together and he drove off. He left us on the shoulder of a dirt road winding narrowly between the bushes, alone with our gear and a pile of baby trees under a tarp.

Ben pulled the tarp off of the cache of seedlings, and we dropped to our knees and began to sort. We ripped open the white-plastic bags, dug our blackened fingers in and pulled out wads of trees by the handful. The moldy ones were slimy grey and limp, and we made gunky piles of them on the gravel. The deadest trees were wet black and coated in stuff that looked like cobwebs.

When we found green springy stems, still living, we tossed them into our planting bags. We rummaged, dumped, tore open new bundles. There was slime on our leathery hands, there was the sun inching inexorably upwards and there was silence apart from the flies.

The two of us shared a little piece of clearcut that day—a little section of mown-down land still surrounded by trees on all sides. We took everything we could carry off the road-side and we walked in, a couple hundred metres through a belt of still-standing forest. Our planting bags were filled with the green stems that we'd salvaged, and we carried the other unopened bundles, one in each fist. We wore back-packs for food-et-cetera and we tucked our shovels hori-zontal through the straps against our backs. We shared my six-litre waterskin between the two of us, and left his gas jerry on the road.

I followed Ben's footsteps exactly, putting my feet where his left off, weaving heavily through the trees until the land fell open into a mashed-up plain of no-longer-forest. At the edge of it we dropped our bags, unsmiling, and we took our shovels each by the handle. We both put music in our ears and headed in opposite directions. I was working from the right and he was working from the left, and the land would be finished once we met in the middle: the land would be covered completely with pine seedlings, each spaced two metres from the next.

The blackflies were just beginning to come out, bouncing off our cheeks and lips, still harmless. The sky was sharp blue and wide open. I was bent over and stabbing at the ground, and taking two steps, and stabbing again, stabbing at bits of earth between the fallen trunks and stumps, rocks, branches, grass and growing things just beginning to turn green.

I'd worked with Ben before, two years earlier. We'd lived and worked together, we'd traveled together, we'd known each other well enough. Well enough, maybe, that there wasn't much left to say by now. Ben was the camp highballer, this season: he was the fastest tree planter in the camp. His days were consumed in a frenzy of caffeine pills and relentless, high-power competition.

Two steps at a time—one tree, two steps, and another tree. High-contrast landscape: black shadows behind blinding white stumps, with the sun uncloaked by anything, baking my brain inside its plastic hard-hat oven. One tree, two steps, and again. Head down, eyes half-closed.

I planted the trees that were in my bags, and loaded up again, and planted them out again, and then again I picked my way back to where we'd dropped our gear. Ben was there already. He was standing and consuming a sandwich with that same relentless concentration—highballer mode—and he told me—

There's no trees.

He'd already walked out to the road, and then back in, and his planting bags were empty and there were no trees for us. We'd planted all the seedlings and Konrad hadn't dropped any more; there was no cache anywhere in sight.

Ben, almost physically vibrating with tension:

No fucking trees—he picked his shovel up—I'm going to wait on the road, he said.

Meanwhile I dropped my shovel. I said:

Well,

And then I leaned over and rummaged in my backpack for a granola bar, while Ben stomped off rustling through the bushes. I followed, eventually, swervingly, chewing.

On the road there was silence. Ben stood silently vibrating and I sat cross-legged drawing lines in the dirt.

A minute went by, and another, and a few more after that. We waited—

No trees: no trees meant no money. No money—

A few minutes is a long, long time for a highballer.

Our crew boss arrived after not-very-long. The rattling van drowned out the buzzing flies and then Konrad was jumping out and tossing bundles of trees out in front of us, and Ben was marching around the van to grab more, and I was just standing up and watching. The only thing Konrad said was,

Is that going to be enough?

Ben nodded affirmative, and there was a big pile of white bundles on the roadside now, and Ben paused a half-second and then said—

Fuck—

And his words went ripping out, words fast and sharp, saying,

Konrad you keep fucking me over—Look I don't care if you leave me in the land without food and water, Fine, but don't fucking leave me without any trees—

And Konrad wasn't smiling, for once. For once, he was devoid of that endless good-natured grin. He was getting back in the van and driving off, and Ben was dropping to his knees and bagging up: ripping bundles open, shoving seedlings into his planting bags.

I pulled a couple bundles from the pile and knelt down, too, and I started smiling and said to Ben,

I can't believe you yelled at Konrad—Poor Konrad—

And Ben glanced up and he almost smiled back, and said, I think I scared him.

I laughed—He'll be alright—

I laughed and Ben almost smiled, and we shrugged into our bags, grabbed more trees, went stomping back in.

It took about eight hours before we met in the middle of our piece of land. Then the jack pine was everywhere, the land was finished, and we shouldered our gear and walked out. Konrad found us on the road and picked us up and moved us each somewhere new for the final hours of the day.

By then we'd killed my six litres of water and I spent the final hours getting slowly sunfucked. The sky was still bare and far too bright, the air was far too still and it was far too early in the season to be ready for that kind of heat.

Sunfucked, or heatfucked: it was a dark-red pounding in the head and the acrid taste of rust in the throat, and everything sounding tinny, vision tilting, thoughts swimming painfully slow.

At the end of the day the van barrelled up to my cache, and I crawled into the backseat and went fully limp. My eyes were open but blankly, peeled and burning and absolutely vacant as we clattered along along the logging road.

Which is why I didn't see it at first—I wasn't looking—

Not until I heard this commotion coming from in front of me: from the twelve young men pressed shoulder-to-shoulder in front of me—suddenly—

Holy fuck,

What the fuck, and

FUCK.

And that was when I really opened my eyes and looked out the window, and that was when I saw one of our school buses lying sideways in the roadside ditch.

It was a strange thing to see. It was a little bit surreal — and that was the only thing that struck me, at first: just that it looked strange. The bus—suddenly it was absolutely massive— It was like seeing a whole building upside-down. Ungainly and unfathomably heavy, dead in the bushes with its oversized wheels upturned overhead —

My second thought, immediately, was this unbidden mental image: fifteen human bodies crumpling like ragdolls against that steel roof as it rolled.

Konrad was speaking into the van's two-way radio, asking the other crew bosses —

Is everyone okay —

And the answer came back that no one was hurt. The emergency brake had failed and the bus had rolled off the road of its own accord, empty, and tipped into the ditch.

Konrad hit the gas, then, carried us away from the roadside spectacle, and we all kept craning our necks to watch the steel corpse recede behind us. Then the commotion got louder and people started to laugh about it, started to joke already.

In camp it was a topic of talk for a while. Rumours swam around over the breakfast tables and in the dinner queue: the bus was uninjured, the bus had been towed into town and it was going to rejoin us tomorrow—no, the next day—no, the *next* day—

And after enough days had gone by, we all accepted that the bus wasn't coming back to camp. We were down one vehicle, and we shuffled to the block and back with two crews sharing the remaining bus, or with one crew riding in the deliverer trucks.

And after enough days had gone by, the sideways school bus was a joke like pretty much everything else.

5

We had a Day Off on Day 11. We spent ten long days in the bush, and then we went into town after work on Day 10. We spent the night in a motel, we hit up the only bar in town, and after that we were permanently disbarred from both the motel and the bar, so we didn't spend any more nights there after that.

Tom told us the reasons behind our disinvitation from the town of Chapleau, and the reasons went something like this —

From the motel: dirty towels; noise complaints; spilled drinks on the carpets, bedsheets, dressers; vomit on the towels, vomit in the bathtub, vomit in the bedsheets; two broken bedframes; one mashed-in ceiling.

From the town bar: empty cans on the lawn; three broken pool cues; one toilet clogged with a full roll of toilet paper; one washroom door off its hinges; one happy couple caught copulating in the closet.

I don't know much about that—any of it. All I know is that I woke up in a motel room, when the door went banging open and Tom came in saying he needed one of the crew bosses to drive him to the clinic because he'd dislocated his shoulder again. And I rolled over to face the wall and groaned to myself while crippled by a headache and some devastating nausea-fatigue. I closed my eyes and tried to stop being conscious, and by the time I dragged myself upright, the only person left in the room was Stefan. He was sitting up in the other bed, using a laptop, and he said smiling,

Good morning.

I staggered across the room and opened the door to try and put air in my lungs, and then I looked outside and said,

Yo, since when is there a fucking river in the parking lot—

And Stefan informed me that I was, in fact, at the River-side Motel.

What the fuck, I said, and I walked out the door.

I went stumbling across Chapleau trying to find the other motel, the one where most of the planters had spent the night—where I'd paid, the previous evening, to split a room with five other girls. On my way there I somehow got lost within the tiny grid of flat streets in between, and I finally arrived at the motel in a state of total disrepair. I threw the door open, threw myself on a bed. The girls were there—five girls I'd met ten days earlier—and I lay there hotly shaking with alcohol, and I started talking at Megan.

It was the first conversation we ever had, and it was mostly one-sided, and it mostly consisted of me saying, over and over again:

This is the only thing we have to look forward to—Lying hungover on a bed—

Megan just laughed so I told her again,

Two more fucking months—This is the only thing to look forward to—Lying hungover on a bed—Two more fucking months—

We spent another two weeks working the clearcuts around Chapleau, after that, and we weren't invited back to that motel. Which is why I can now say that the longest I've ever gone without showering was a solid sixteen days. To be fair, I did jump in a river twice within that interval, so perhaps it doesn't count.

6

Our first Camp Move was on Day 16. We woke up at 6 am to Ceilidh the cook bombing around the campsite leaning on the horn of Tom's pickup truck. We tore down camp in a gambolling manner, pulling apart the steel ribcage of the mess tent, folding up the tarps, packing the six shitters into a tow trailer and filling in holes, filling in holes — six shitter holes and the slurry pit — filling in holes with the dry gravel stuff of the empty quarry where we'd been living. Cook shack, gas cache, dry tent: packed up and moved in a shuffling set of busloads and trailer-hauling pickup trucks to the Watershed.

There, the same process in reverse — unpacking, unfolding, clipping together and re-constructing, and digging holes, digging holes.

Stefan and Arron and Yukon and I were sipping beers on top of a cliff when Vanessa found us and told us to come dig a hole. Early evening, lowering light, bouncy clouds of insects. We'd set up most of the camp and our own personal tents, and we had our second Night Off to look forward to.

The four of us were perched at the top of this steep sandy fir-crested slope, and spread out below us were the white-tarp half-barrels of the mess tent and dry tent, and the last remaining school bus and the trucks and the vans. In a little bare corner, huddled up against the trees, the six plastic shitter-boxes were set up like cheap green telephone booths so close together the doors knocked against each other if they were opened at the same time.

Arron and Stefan and I camped together at the edge of that sandy cliff. Yukon didn't because he slept in his truck, but we were all up there, sipping beer together and dangling our legs off the edge, when we were spotted by the assistant cook, Vanessa. She called up to us, told us to come down. She wanted us to dig the slurry pit: a big hole in the ground two metres by two metres by two metres, beside the cook shack trailer. Obediently we followed her to the spot — same place every year — and we continued sipping beers, and we kicked at the hard-packed earth, pushed some rocks this way and that, and Yukon asked Vanessa — Where are the axes?

Haven't been unloaded yet, she said,
So he asked in his gravelly voice, half-smiling —
Can we dig the pit later, when we're drunk and have axes?
Vanessa rolled her eyes — Do you think that's a good idea?
So we dug the pit later, when we were drunk and had axes.

That was an in-camp Night Off — far from the constraints of civilization, in that little grassy clearing in the woods. Sixty or so bush-people, only sixteen days in. There were wilderness-sized drinking sports: Beersbee (involved frisbees) and Basebeer (baseball bats) and Bottle Toss (garbage cans). The wooden posts on the highway were getting replaced and somehow the old wood was donated to us so we made a mad high bonfire out of it. That was the night Devon's nose was broken by a baseball bat, but that was an accident, and Tom was sober, took him to the hospital — no harm done.

Yukon and I sat by the bonfire and had to keep backing up our chairs because the inferno was so hot on the face. We sat there all night, catching up and discussing plans —

Plans, already, for when we got out of that godforsaken bush camp — and it was only sixteen days in. We were talking about mountains; Yukon was talking about escaping into the mountains —

I can't fucking wait, he said — already.

And he said, I know exactly where I'm going, As soon as this is over, I've found the place.

We leaned back in our white plastic chairs side-by-side, and we watched from across the pile of burning posts while a macho drunk guy got a bunch of highballers worked up. This guy was a newcomer—he'd just arrived to the camp, a couple weeks late, and now he was noisily claiming to be the best planter around. He started spewing out these overloud assertions, these tactless taunts straight at Ben the highballer and two of his high-production peers.

The guys started to get their hackles up, started to throw insults and accusations—voices getting loud, louder—

I turned to Yukon and raised my eyebrows.

This looks violent, I said, It's kind of uncomfortable.

And that was when I saw him grinning madly, orange fire glinting on his teeth—and him saying, No—Let him talk—I fucking love this shit—

Alright, okay—I leaned back in my chair and watched the soused-up men tensing their muscles and putting steel into their voices, and the whole time Yukon was there silently laughing and gleeful with it.

The cocky newcomer was outnumbered anyway and he started to get quieter the more obvious that became. The flames started to get lower over the mounds of red-hot embers and everything was simmering down, and eventually the new guy walked away.

I did too—I walked away to find more beer where I'd cached it in the back of Konrad's van. And then I stopped to look up at the stars, outside the glow of the bonfire—because on a clear night, out there, the depth of the sky turns the forest into a cardboard cutout by comparison. But that night I looked up at the sky and the stars were already gone, and instead there was the cold glow of dawn, and then that old dread came back—

I took my last beer up the crumbling slope to my tent, and I crawled inside and hid from the oncoming day.

About four hours later, we were heading into Chapleau for our Day Off. We weren't allowed in the motel or the bar, but we still crowded into the dank yellow room behind the corner store to circle like vultures around the laundry machines.

Chapleau: a town of about two thousand people, a little less than a thousand kilometres northwest of Toronto. A grid of low wide streets based around the intersection of a highway and a railyard. Traffic in Chapleau was made of pickup trucks and quads. It had truckers' motels, one Legion bar, a supermarket, a couple of eateries and two hardware stores.

For us, the main attractions were the poutine stand, the thrift shop, and the library by the river.

We didn't go into the library that day. We spread ourselves out in the parking lot under the heavy cloudy sky and the sprinkling rain. It was voting day, and the residents of Chapleau were filing in and out of the library to fill their ballots and meanwhile we were staggering about half-drunk on the dandelion-splattered lawn out back, holding towels up for each other and undressing. We were feverishly consuming bags of candy, and ice cream and poutine, trying to quell that sharp-clawed hunger that would never quite leave us alone. We were padding around barefoot in our underwear, off the lawn and onto the flooded dock, into the dark icy water. Planting our feet on the slippery black wood between the thick black leeches. Off the edge of the dock, the river stung in our open cuts, stung our burning forearms crisscrossed with thin red lines, and the river chilled the bugbites, calmed and cooled, felt so fresh that we came out grinning and laughing. Laughing and coughing, because everyone was sick with something—but nothing too serious, just these angry phlegmy coughs that kept echoing around. We came out with our hands and arms black-and-red, and the rest of us white-and-purple, pale legs all ravaged with bruises and bites. We came out and scrubbed ourselves, scrubbed each other, tried to get some of the blackness out of the creases in our skin — but some of it was permadirt, of course, just like permahunger: permanent until the planting was finished, and finished for long enough that our bodies could try to forget about it.

7

Those were our two Day Offs at the Watershed. The same story, Day 17 and Day 23:

An overlong fiery night, a burning hangover and a frigid dip in the river to try and put it out.

Day 23, after the second communal bath behind the Chapleau library, Arron and Stefan and I cooked steak. We sauteed it in beer in my baking pan over Arron's propane cooker, and we turned it over with Stefan's multitool pliers, while huddling in sweaters against the bugs and the air on top of our cliff above the Watershed.

We went to sleep soon afterwards—an early night in preparation for another long week. I crawled inside the layers of blankets on the floor of my tent, lay my head down on a rolled-up sweater and tucked my nose into my sleeping bag, away from the cold in the air. In the silence then, I heard a popping sound like rain against the fly of my tent. Eyes closed, I listened, and I knew it wasn't raining.

My lullaby that night was the sound of the blackflies finally coming out in full force. It was the sound of a horde caught under the fly of my tent, bouncing around in their carnivorous clouds as thick as falling rain.

The clouds of bugs were so stunning the next day that I stopped planting trees for a few seconds just to absorb the spectacle of it.

I stopped with one hand on my shovel, and the other hand on my nose, and my back horizontal to the swamp. I'd paused—which is a heresy, you know—you should never, ever pause—

I'd paused to indulge in the pleasure of shooting thick wads of gunk out of one nostril at a time. It was part of the sickness that was bouncing around camp, this illness that we kept joking about—this virus or whatever it was, jumping from one person to the next and gaining momentum so that first it was just a cold, and then someone added a cough and someone added a fever and the next thing would be sudden death—

I was shooting thick dollops of mucus out of the right side of my nose, and slowly leaking orange fluid out of the left. I thought that maybe it was brain fluid, leaking out of my nose, and I thought that if my brain leaked out it might be less boring to plant trees all day so I didn't really mind that. And I paused, heretically, to shoot some phlegm out, and that was when I looked down. My boots were half-invisible in black water and my shovelblade deep in black muck and I had one black stinging hand pressed against my left nostril — and that was when I found that the air in front of me wasn't air at all — but was some oscillating greyness instead — some shimmering storm of biting insects and that was when I really noticed them. That was when I really noticed the fact that there were blackflies biting chunks out of my bare arms, and blackflies crawling up my sleeves into my armpits, blackflies landing on my lips, nestling into the corners of my eyes, blackflies bombing into the collar of my shirt, inviting themselves inside of my bra, and just one blackfly screaming madly inside of my ear — and I paused and thought that maybe I was in a horror movie, and I had nowhere to go, nowhere to escape to, and this cloud of insects was going to devour me one bite at a time. There was a hole in my leggings — a dime-sized hole on my right thigh where the blackflies had found flesh and found blood and now they were eating my leg and the flowing blood had begun to form a sticky crust, and the clumsy seedlike bodies of the flies were getting stuck in it, and more of them were arriving to burrow between the red-spattered corpses of their comrades, and I watched this spectacle with a kind of horrified amazement, and I had nowhere to go and nowhere to escape to and still they were swarming and still they were crawling on my neck and buzzing in my ears —

So I stopped pausing, then, and pulled my bandana lower over my ears, and put a tree in the ground where my shovel had been, kept my eyes half-closed and looked at the ground two metres away and put a tree there too.

8

The ride home was an hour and a half long, dampish and burnt-out on bugspray. Heads lolling limply, feet and fingers pruny with swamp, necks and arms speckled with scabby red bites. When we got back to camp I fled the sticky cage of the van and went hands-and-feet scrambling in the sand to get up onto our cliff. Past Arron's tent perched right on the edge, and into the glade where mine was tucked away. I peeled off my swamp-soaked layers of boot, sock, pant, and hung the clothes on some boughs of fir and I slid with relief into a couple of dry-ish sweaters and thermal socks, sweatpants and loose sneakers. Made my way back down for dinner, after that — carefully, clumpily placing each aching foot, one at a time down the side of that steep-steep slope.

An hour-and-a-half commute, the following day, too. Day 25, our crew was scattered across a sprawling set of cut blocks, and half of our planters rode home on the remaining bus instead. Those of us in the van happily capitalized on the vacant seats to make ourselves ever-more horizontal — slumping sideways and closing our eyes against the itchiness, the damp and the hunger. We reached the camp and I escaped again into the comfort of my collapsible home — immediately.

So then when I came clumping-sliding down the sandy cliffside, dryly clothed, Konrad found me and he was annoyed. He was still smiling, because Konrad was always smiling — almost, almost always — but he was annoyed at me too.

He accosted me at the base of the sandhill and said smiling accusationally:

You always run away before I can get your tallies — You and Arron both — I need your tallies, okay, If you want to get paid.

I grinned at him. The day was over and my clothes were dry — so I grinned gladly and I gave him my tallies.

Tallies means how many trees I'd planted that day. The crew bosses kept track of our numbers, so that we could be paid per tree later on. At the end of each day, we would each count out the white plastic bags from each of the bundles we'd planted — count the empty bags and then shove them into garbage bags and then throw them into a pile, and later move the pile into the garbage trailer and later throw it on the ground at the dump.

I told Konrad my number of empty plastic bags, and he made a note in his binder, and then he glanced up the hill to Arron's tent and told me —

Go up there and get Arron, I need his tallies too.

And I grinned and said,

That hill is the hardest part of my day, I'm not going back up there —

And I moved off towards the mess tent, off to find my baking pan among the clutter of mismatched dishes in the racks, and off to join the salivating queue of planters shuffling up towards the ladles of the cooks —

And meanwhile, Konrad-barely-smiling went trudging up that hill. He shook Arron's tent and called Arron's name, and that's when he discovered that Arron wasn't in his tent — and that's when he discovered that Arron wasn't in camp at all — because, as it turned out, Arron was actually stranded alone on the block.

9

Arron was the one who brought me tree planting in the first place. He and I attended the same university. Once, when I was in my second year of university, when I was indoors and fresh and dry and clean, I was standing up at a desk and looking at a blank piece of paper, and Arron walked up to me and said this:

Of everyone here, I think you're the only one who could be a tree planter.

And I smiled, and said, Cool.

Let me know if you want a job, he told me.

But I didn't want a job, and in fact, what I really thought was this:

Why the fuck would anyone want to be a tree planter?

Arron had become a tree planter after his first year in university. He was Konrad's roommate. Konrad's older sister had been a highballer, and she'd recommended Konrad to the job, and he'd brought Arron along, and so they'd both gone to work in the bush at the age of eighteen.

That year, the two of them were the camp's rookie highballers. Each in their own way — Arron with his lean-muscled agility, and Konrad with his broad-shouldered strength. Both were prodigious athletes, and both were motivated by competing with each other.

Arron and Konrad and I all went to the same university, same department, same age. We were all nineteen at the end of our second school year, when Arron and Konrad returned for their second season of tree planting, and I tagged along for my first.

I really hated it. I was really bad at it, too. The whole thing was terrible, and it was so much fun that I did it again, and again, and again after that.

10

I didn't know that Arron was stuck on the block that day. I joined the buzzing throng in the mess tent, received a massive heap of food and slumped into a plastic chair, surrounded in close quarters by bubbling dialogue and dirt-streaked faces. Everyone's zombie-stares went gleeful as soon as the food had been dished out.

Pork chops, mashed potatoes, buttered broccoli, salad and fresh bread that evening — everything heavy, salty, rich — thick unlimited food that made us worship our angelic cook Ceilidh. Dinners were dished out by the young assistant cook Vanessa, dished out along with a side of scathing sarcasm or overt indifference —

And we grinned and thanked her as she ladled it out, and then we sat down for the quotidian feast: excessively-laden dishes heavy on the flimsy tables, and all of us crowding our chairs tight against each other, shoveling the food in — fast and urgent in an animal way — because of that *hunger* —

We leaned forward to consume everything, feverishly, and then gradually we leaned back, slumped down, let our legs stretch out, and we laughed about everything, and we relaxed. Comfortable, finally, for the first time all day.

It was then that I began to hear the rumour flitting around. A weightless rumour at first, it started to gain momentum like a whirlpool, started to get heavy and gravitate to the centre of conversation:

Yes, It's true — Arron got left on the block.

I laughed.

Korry asked me: Is he going to be mad?

And I laughed — Arron? I said — I don't think Arron will be mad — I could be wrong, but I don't think so,

And I laughed again.

Though really it wasn't that funny.

We had no way of knowing where he was, or what had happened since he'd been alone. He wasn't in camp: that's all we knew. Konrad and Tom had left immediately, to go back to the block and find him — But until they came back, we had no way of contacting him, no way of knowing where he was, or how.

But there was nothing we could do about it, either.

After dinner people started to trickle out of the mess tent, out to smoke or off to bed. I moved out to wash my pan and fork in the hose-fed sink outside the cook shack, in an orangey liquid that left the dishes greasier post-washing than pre-. I stood outside and brushed my teeth next to the barrels of drinking water propped up alongside the mess tent. I filled up a water canteen so I could try to hydrate myself, and gradually I rolled back into the mess tent and I sat to wait for Arron, or I sat to wait for news of Arron.

There was no other way of knowing — and I had to know, you know.

11

Lack of communication was what left him stranded that evening. It was an honest mistake and an unlikely one. In my experience, this had never happened before.

Konrad's planters were scattered across a lot of land and mixed up with another crew. Arron had been dropped off at the edge of the block, at the back end of a logging road. He was working in an oblong slice of land that reached deep into the treeline, and he'd asked one of the deliverers to move his cache of seedlings off the road, closer to the area where he was planting.

At the end of the day, the last remaining school bus rolled down the logging road to collect the mixed crew of planters who were working there. Arron's cache wasn't visible from the road, and neither was Arron. So while Konrad assumed that Arron would be picked up by the bus, the bus-driving crew boss assumed that Arron was already on the van. And both vehicles rolled off without him.

At 6 pm Arron's watched beeped to tell him that the day was over. He'd emptied his bags of seedlings and he was cleaning up his cache for the night, collecting the empty plastic bags and pulling the tarp over the remaining bundles. He picked up his shovel, backpack, gas jerry, and he walked out across the land. Boots and socks squelching with swampwater and the wind whistling through a damp-filthy shirt. Heavy clouds of water in the sky above and shimmering clouds of black-flies in droves all around.

He walked across the land, eyes down, high-stepping obstacles. He crested a gentle hill at the edge of the clearcut and he looked out over the logging road, looked for the bus that was bringing him home.

He looked out and his heart skipped a beat and started to pound, hard.

There was no bus, of course. There were no planters. There were no human beings.

There was instead an empty gravel road winding narrowly between vast sprawling clearcuts, and there were caches carefully cleaned and covered in tarps for the night. And on all horizons there was a deep black treeline — wild forests thick, dark, endless — and the sun slowly-steadily sinking down.

12

Hours passed by. I waited for Arron in the mess tent. The sun kept sinking until the forests around the Watershed were liquid black, a spiky ring framing clouds above. The mess tent glowed ghostlike in the darkness: a forty-foot long half-cylinder, cloaked in white tarp with its steel ribs showing through. The open flaps at either end cast light onto the hard-packed earth outside — deep yellow light from two rows of lightbulbs strung up along the inner walls.

I sat with Korry and Mandog at a plastic table under the bare incandescents, while everything quieted down and emptied out. I sat waiting.

Waiting: waiting was the only thing that ever lifted the weight of constant urgency. Planting, eating, sleeping, drinking — these things were always urgent; there would never be enough time. The only moment of rest, of real justified inactivity, came while waiting. So I waited, melted into a plastic chair, and I grinned about it.

Korry and Mandog were rookies on my crew that season. The three of us sat in a fluctuating silence while Korry mended a hole in Mandog's pants and Mandog entertained himself with ambient mosquitoes. He was snatching them from the air, one a time, and carefully painstakingly skewering them onto Korry's extra sewing needles. He made three mosquito skewers that looked like tiny spruce trees: upright needle-trunks with flimsy radii of legs and wings and proboscises.

And casually, inside of the quietude of that evening, Mandog showed us his arm. He pulled back the sleeve of his jacket, placed his forearm on the table, soft side up, and said:

Check it out, I think a bug laid eggs in my arm.

Which was not the correct diagnosis, in fact. The thing he showed us that night was not a cache of bug-eggs; it was an infection. It was the first time I'd ever seen one of these things, but later they would become an all-too-familiar sight. Later these infections would sweep through the camp like a plague, and later there would be medications prescribed and there would be emergency-room visits and there would be hospitalization and surgery — and eventually, much later, there would be an actual diagnosis.

But we didn't know any of that, Day 25. We didn't know what this thing was. Mandog said,

I think a bug laid eggs in my arm,

And we leaned over to take a look at it.

A hard raised bump in the middle of his forearm, perhaps a centimetre in diameter, and red, with the skin stretched tight over it and the first layer peeling off.

We didn't know for sure, but someone decided that it needed to be popped, and Korry performed surgery. She dipped the end of one sewing needle in antibacterial gel, and pricked at the swollen lump.

It was disgusting and fascinating in the way that these things are. First Mandog squeezed it and there was just a bit of bloody water trickling out. Squeezed harder and then all of a sudden there came a pea-sized spurt of yellowy-whiteness like toothpaste sliding out, wetly, thick and ugly. Korry wiped it up with gauze and was convinced that there was more so she kept squeezing. Mandog's teeth were clenched and he swore a bit because it fucking hurt, and his forearm was going splotchy red from the pressure, and the sore was trickling blood. Eventually we decided that all of the toothpaste-stuff was out so Korry bandaged it with gauze and tape and antibacterial cream. Mandog pulled his sleeve back down, leaned back.

Gradually the quietude blanketed us again. Korry finished sewing, and she slid all the dead insects off of her needles onto the table, packed up her sewing kit, and the two of them swayed away to their tents.

A set of headlights lit up the blackness outside and I strode out to meet them — but it wasn't Arron, that time. It was Yukon and Stefan coming home from a late gas-station run. I went back into the mess tent. I sat. I sipped on cold plasticky water. I waited.

13

Arron waited at the roadside until a quarter to seven. That was part of his plan.

It was like this —

He saw the empty road spread out below him, and his heart skipped a beat and there was the option of panicking.

But then, there is often the option of panicking. Out there, when you are alone all the time, and the weather is against you and the land is against you, and there is no one around to tell you what to do or to even act like they care, and there is always that crushing sense of urgency —

Panicking is often an option. And eventually you learn that panicking doesn't really help.

Arron's heart skipped a beat, and he paused, and he thought, and then he started to make plans.

He waited by the roadside until 6:45 in case Konrad was still on his way, just running late. In the meantime he took stock of what he had with him:

He still had some water in his gas jerry, and in his backpack he had a pocketknife and an iPod, an empty lunch container, a pack of cigarettes and a light rain shell, some hockey tape, pen and paper. He was annoyed that he'd forgotten to bring a lighter, because he might have liked to start a fire, and far more urgently he'd have liked to have a cigarette.

He planned to wait until it was closer to dusk. If he was still there, alone, as the sun was setting, then he would gather wood and kindling, which wouldn't be difficult to find in a place like that. He would generate a spark by stabbing the knife through the battery of his ipod. He would take off his wet boots and socks, and wrap his feet with the dry sleeves of his shirt and with hockey tape, then wrap his body with tarps from the roadside caches, and then lie by the fire to wait out a very long, very cold and very lonely night — which besides being merely unpleasant was also going to be seriously dangerous due to the unpredictability of both the weather and the wildlife —

In the meantime, there was still the chance that he would be remembered and returned for before nightfall.

And that was all he had: an indefinite waiting game.

He sat alone on the road. Silence.

Silence, blackflies, wind. Wind in the tree branches — distantly rustling the face of that endless treeline — and once in a while an extra-forceful gust that perfectly mimicked the sound of a vehicle rolling down a gravel road.

And then silence. And hunger, and an ever-more penetrating chill in the air, and that half-deadly exhaustion. And each minute drawing itself out, longer —

This is what Arron did, then:

He filled his bags up with trees, walked back into the land, bent down and put seedlings in the ground, one at a time, for two and half hours more.

14

That's where he was, when Tom and Konrad rolled up in the F350. It was after 9 pm by then, and Arron was out in the land still wearing a hard hat and a high-visibility vest and moving steadily along as though the workday had never ended.

They laughed at him about that — about wearing the Client-enforced PPE, with no one else around — but they were laughing with actual gladness and with actual relief. They both got out of the truck to give him a hug. Tom and Konrad apologized profusely, but still the three of them were smiling about it, and laughing too because of that real delighted high. The best part, Arron told me, was that Tom had brought him a heaping container of dinner for the hour-and-a-half ride home.

Back at camp he was a war hero. It was late and black outside and most of the camp had gone to sleep, but there was a core of veterans who were up and waiting. Tom's headlights splintered the darkness, barrelling in from the highway, and then there were celebrations in order. A circle formed — Arron, Tom, Konrad, Yukon, Stefan, Parks, Gabe — and laughter echoed out — ferocious hugs and pats on the back, and all the voices raised to recapitulate with enthusiasm. There was that kind of deliverance at the end of every day for us — but some days more than others.

I waited at the base of our sandhill and watched the group silhouetted in the headlights until Arron broke away — smiling still and dragging his feet after the eighteen-hour workday.

You're still awake! he said to me, and I hugged him, smiling, said,

I had to be awake to make sure you were alive.

We clambered uphill together. On top of the slope I wrapped myself in blankets and went horizontal, and I listened to the empty sky with the loon calls echoing through it and I listened to the gentle rustling of the fir trees. I listened to the blackflies popping against the fabric, and to Arron and Stefan zipping their tents for the night, and I lay down to embrace unconsciousness —

Then through the open darkness, Arron's voice came floating; he called out to us —

Hey guys? he said, Thanks for waiting up for me.

And Stefan smiled — I heard the smile, I swear —

Good to have you back, he said.

15

When I went tree planting for the first time, it wasn't because I wanted to go tree planting. It was more because I had nothing else to be doing, and because the world was making me claustrophobic and I had to escape somehow.

When Arron approached me in our second year of university, I'd been about to drop out of school. It was February; spring was approaching and the dull season of education would be over soon enough. Then as summer rolled in I would be scrounging around for some kind of irrelevant low-wage job and then spending four months grinding away my daytimes in order to pay off another season of school —

And then after that was over I was supposed to go scrounging around again for some kind of entry-level employment in order to pay rent somewhere so that I could sleep in the same place every night and wake up in the same place every morning, spend the days watching the clock tick itself out over and over again and then go to sleep in the same place every night, and wake up again and so on —

And the sheer predictability of it was closing in around me, and I was there thinking to myself, To hell with it, and I decided to flee the country.

Arron's job offer was a sudden escape route. I thought maybe if I went through with this thing, then maybe I wouldn't have to worry about the money, and also maybe it would burn out some of the wanderlust and then maybe I'd be able to go through with the rest of my schooling — as prudence advised. So that was why I chased after Arron and told him,

Yes, can you please get me a job.

As I've said, it was terrible and it was the hardest thing I'd ever done but at least it wasn't boring — at least, not in the same way that real life is boring — and what's really important is that it's very hard to be claustrophobic in a clearcut.

Tom's the one who hired me, in a long-distance video interview. I dressed for it, tried to look like a respectable stand-up person, although my head was shaved in some kind of a mohawk at the time. And I was nervous but then the video opened and Tom was there lounging on a bed and speaking with his long Canadian drawl, his face obscured by hair-and-beard. Tom would cut his hair roughly once every two years; during the interview it was shoulder-length, and at the beginning of that season it was cropped short, and during my third season it was shoulder-length again.

He conducted the interview by describing all the ways in which tree planting was a terribly challenging and oft-unpleasant occupation, and then he asked me if I was still interested in pursuing it.

And smiling I said, Oh it sounds great.

When I was hired, I didn't know what a clearcut looked like, and I never really stopped to think about it. Somehow in the back of my mind, in those months approaching May, I was envisioning a quiet sun-dappled forest and all the healthful benefits of fresh air and exercise.

Which in hindsight, of course, is either quite sad or laughable. But as the saying goes, live and learn.

So on my first day of tree planting, I learned what a clearcut looked like, and I was afraid — I mean, I was truly afraid, to such a degree that it was almost sickening.

We drove to work in a school bus that had a portrait of the Virgin Mary duct-taped above the windshield, gazing demurely over the rows of ragged seats. Above the door, just right of the Blessed Mother, there was more duct tape which spelled out spiky capital letters and an arrow and it said WELCOME TO HELL and the arrow pointed down to the open door, which in turn framed a frigid slice of clearcut and a white tarp over a cache of trees on the ground.

And it was, yeah, it was the closest I'd ever come to being in hell, all day every day.

Here's what I discovered:

A clearcut isn't a sun-dappled forest, and it isn't a farmer's field. It's a wild shredded terrain that's massive and churned up and it completely dwarfs the little human specks that go crawling around inside of it like tiny bacteria in a festering sore.

Tree planters don't spend their days strolling across cool fields of soft brown earth. They spend their days fighting, tearing, kicking and splashing, and at the end of the day they come out bruised and ragged, with eyes that burn blankly ahead because the mind is gone and the body is too tired to blink.

That's how it is. A clearcut can be a varied terrain but it is very rarely an easy one. There are turned-up logs strewn across it with the roots towering above, nets of tangled branches to climb through, icy black moats thigh-deep, and slippery mud that blows the knees out. There are house-sized boulders cracked by fire, and sheer cliffsides hard and crumbling. There are fields of shoulder-high thorns stretching to every horizon, and whipping branches and hornets' nests — and tree planters go barreling through it all and they learn to enjoy pain.

On my first day it was snowing, lightly.

I planted about seventy trees. I earned about six dollars.

At the end of the day, every day, Camp Cost was taken off of each planter's paycheck to cover the cost of food and gasoline: Camp Cost was about twenty-three dollars.

Beyond the inherent difficulty of carrying a third or half your own body mass in added weight and moving nonstop for ten hours and doing the same motions on repeat with all of the force you can muster —

Beyond that, well, sometimes you get lost. Or at least, I got lost. I got lost so much that it was downright embarrassing.

On my first day they told us this:

Plant trees, two metres apart from each other, all over your piece of land, with every tree tight and deep and upright in mineral soil.

Mineral soil? I found rocks and moss and sticks, brambles and decaying organic matter, but I didn't find any soil. Haphazardly I put trees in the ground as deep as I could manage to, and then I lost track of the trees themselves and I couldn't remember what direction I was supposed to be walking in, so then I went meandering in these slow jagged zigzags, stumbling over the seedlings I'd already planted, and every time I stood up to get my bearings everything rearranged itself and all those tiny hand-length stems disappeared completely into the chaos of the landscape and I had no idea where I was or what I was doing.

I staggered around kicking my shovel desperately into the ground, because I couldn't muster enough force with my arm alone, and it might have been one hour or five before my crew boss found me. Amo arrived on foot, walking the land between all the rookies — rookies, who had flooded the camp and outnumbered the veterans — and he found all my invisible trees and followed them to me and tugged on them, pulled them up and said,

These are some of the worst trees I've ever seen.

So everything was off to a pretty bad start, and that went on for a while.

As a rookie I cried three times, and each time I continued planting trees, and multitasked by crying and planting at the same time.

Once I cried because my planting bags had rubbed the skin off of my hips, so that at the end of the day I had to peel my t-shirt out of these bloody pussing sores above the waistband of my pants, and the next day with every step the weight of the trees kept ripping the scabs off and then ripping deeper, and I was determined to hit a Personal Best that day, so I did, but with tears coming out of my eyes for the first few hours until everything went numb.

Once I cried because I was lost desperately in a swamp and the Client's quality checker came by and told me that my trees were too wet and I had to re-plant them, so I kept moving but when he left my land I silently cried to myself, and when my crew boss came by I paused to glare at him, stony, red-eyed, and told him to get out of my land, and he did.

Once I cried when I didn't see anyone else all day and I was actually thinking about something completely irrelevant which might not have been such a big deal if I hadn't been so entirely exhausted, hungry, thirsty, and overwhelmed, so that the memories of another lifetime brought tears to my eyes, and then I just kept planting trees until my thoughts went away.

And I could say more about all the pain and all the different types of suffering, but with time all of that becomes routine and eventually you know that none of it is really unbearable, and regardless of anything there's nothing to do but just keep planting trees.

After my rookie season, I did break down and cry just once more, two years later hunched over a gravel road under a cloudy sky and very much alone. But that had less to do with the tree planting itself and more to do with all these escalating circumstances that started when I broke one of my legs in half by accident.

But all of that came later.

16

The Client we worked for, this season, was a paper/pulp/lumber company that cut down a bunch of trees and was therefore required to replace them. The cut blocks had once been natural-growth forests of mixed hardwood and softwood, and they had been harvested for the softwood alone. The Client hired our Company to replace the forests with a monoculture, or sometimes a mix, of spruce and/or pine.

After sixty to eighty years, the trees we planted will be old enough to get cut down again.

I can't speak for everyone, but I generally had the impression that none of us spent very much time thinking about that.

We received the seedlings from the tree nursery. They were delivered to the camp in loads of about three hundred thousand at a time, hauled along the highway by a semi and dropped off in a clearing somewhere between the campsite and the block, in a refrigerated trailer box also referred to as a reefer.

The tree nursery grew the baby trees and then kept them frozen over the winter. By the time we were planting them, in the spring, the trees should have been thawed, but evidently they sometimes had not.

If the trees were still partially frozen when we received them, the ice was generally concentrated at the centre of each bundle — just a handful of pods stuck together in a clump. The Client's instructions were to leave these clumps on the roadside until they thawed completely, and then to carefully separate them and plant them one at a time. The Client would walk around in our land — two or three or four Client representatives, out in the field — and they would supervise us to ensure that we were treating their seedlings with due reverence. Each and every seedling was a monetary investment for the Client.

So when the seedlings arrived in frozen clumps, we would wait patiently and separate the pods with care. We would never try to break the blocks of ice by pounding them to bits with our shovels, nor by smashing them repeatedly against the trunk of a standing tree.

In any case, when the trees arrived partially frozen, this was a relatively minor setback to us — just another small annoyance on top of the many small annoyances associated with the job.

But the frozen trees became a major setback when they weren't just partially frozen — when they were, instead, entirely and unambiguously frozen solid into rock-hard blocks of ice — when they were so frozen that we actually couldn't work for two full days.

And that might have been kind of exciting — to have an unexpected Double Day Off — except that we'd just had two days off, already.

So instead of being excited, then, everyone was getting restless and impatient about the fact that we weren't making any money — because no one wanted to be hanging around in a bush camp without making any money. And also because our endless days of pieceworking were fueled all the time by this panicked sense of urgency, and it was pretty hard to shake that feeling, so everyone was somewhat consumed by this guilt-ridden anxiety over our ten-cents-at-a-time — ten-cents-every-six-seconds — always —

So when we didn't have any trees to plant we weren't really sure what to do with ourselves and everyone got pretty anxious or antsy or angry about it, or at the very least they got pretty drunk.

It was Day 29 when the trees were frozen like that. Tom stood up in the mess tent after dinner to tell us the news and he said he felt terrible about it, absolutely terrible — although it wasn't even remotely his fault. Tom stood at one end of the tent, beside a table of flat cake on flat trays laid out by Ceilidh and Vanessa, and he said,

Alright, guys —

But then a crew boss interrupted and said the whole camp needed to watch Maddie get cakefaced, so the crew boss took a piece of cake and made a mess of it, icing-first against Maddie's face so everyone could cheer and laugh and Maddie was laughing too, and that's what she'd earned by losing a bet.

After that the meeting was allowed to start.

Tom stood and told us that he'd met with the tree nursery and the Client, and that they'd been trying to resolve the problem with the moldy trees.

The spruce seemed to be alright, but the jack pine were fatally moldy. This was becoming a serious issue, because we were planting too many dead trees, which meant the investment would be a dead end, and the Client didn't like that.

So, Tom said, the tree nursery hired a forestry professional to try and discern the source of the mold. And here, Tom was half-smiling about it, and we all started to laugh a bit — and with the laughs, that tenacious chorus of wet hacking coughs — because, said Tom,

I would almost assume that a tree nursery would be run by forestry professionals to begin with, But I guess not, So they had to hire one —

Just one. One professional to help out the poor folks at the nursery.

Dark laughter.

And in any case the hired professional decided that the mold was forming during the thawing process, and that the solution, therefore, was to not thaw the trees whatsoever.

Which was why we received a shipment of three hundred thousand trees that were all frozen solid, and we couldn't do a thing about that and we couldn't do any work for two days, and we were stuck for another two days in a flat charred-up gravel clearing in the bush outside of Timmins, Ontario.

17

At that point we'd just had a Camp Move from the Watershed to the Campground. That was on Day 27, and it was phenomenally exciting because it meant that we could spend a night in Timmins. The Campground was only forty minutes from Timmins, and Timmins was about twenty times the size of Chapleau, and Timmins had lots of things in it, like real beds and hot showers.

So on Day 27 we went into Timmins in high spirits and reacquainted ourselves with the old east wing of that fortress-like hotel, where they segregated all the tree planters and jacked up the prices because it wasn't fair to the real humans to have to put up with our stench and our flailing drunkenness.

Always urgency: even Night Off. Everything was urgent. Six of us in a room, rotating showers. By then it had been sixteen days since anyone had showered at all, and it had been twenty-seven days since anyone had showered with hot water, since Chapleau never had enough to go around. A month in the bush, and now for the first time we each felt the heat lift the stickiness of our skin, soothe the burning of the sun and the scratches and the DEET spray.

The prolonged filthiness was just like anything else — we got used it. It wasn't hard to do. We would go a week or two without showering and we wouldn't be able to smell ourselves or anyone else. Once in a while we might catch a whiff of something strong and earthy, and it wasn't all that bad. Our clothes were muddy, and our skin and bedding were sticky-gritty-damp all the time, and there was a kind of liberation in that, really — because once you are as filthy as you

can possibly be, then you don't have to worry about it anymore. Instead you just embrace it.

At the end of sixteen days, showering was a bit like magic,
and we had all earned the experience of being physically
reborn in a haze of steam and the scent of hotel bath soap,
and everything afterwards felt cloud-soft and delightful.

By then it was evening already and it was our only Night
Off until god-knows-when so we needed to arrange food
and alcohol — urgently — because there was that permahunger always ripping us apart inside, and there was also that
feverish necessity to be terribly and overwhelmingly inebriated.

So, quick, we'd find food and beer or hard liquor, and
once the hunger was satiated then we we would go swirling between the hotel rooms and merging like this obnoxious flood — noise and nonsense escalating, with sixty young
things generating a hot communal frenzy, hyped up on
booze and whatever else could be unearthed — and we would
go flooding into the street like liquid, go pouring into the
club across the road where they let us dance shirtless because
we were fun and we spent a lot of money, and there we
would flood the smoking terrace, the pool tables, the dance
floor — with everyone wild and wide-eyed — and sometimes
it was like we were inhaling and exhaling thoughts and feelings, like we were mixing identities by accident because we
all felt the same all the time, and we all felt completely invincible because that's what it feels like when you are made out
of sixty people instead of just one person like you used to be.

So Night Off could get kind of wild, you know, and it was
easy enough to forget yourself and get swept up in this giddy
rage, and maybe accidentally wind up thinking that there
isn't much that's better than those raucous roaring nights
all imbecilic and adrenaline-crazed in some grungy club in a
dark northern mining town surrounded by a bunch of per-
madirty drunk kids.

And sometimes the nights would end or maybe they wouldn't, and sometimes the sun would just rise too early and find us everywhere, sprawled out or meandering, maybe in hotel rooms tangled three to a bed or maybe in the hotel lobby or out in the streets, in a ditch somewhere or horizontal on a picnic table, or wherever, and whenever, and whatever, and it would just carry on.

Morning, Day 28, Konrad found me to say goodbye and I was in my hotel room like I was supposed to be, overhot and red-eyed with the alcohol and exhaustion. Konrad and I had gone to the poutine stand at 5 am, and now two hours later I'd rediscovered the whole congealed brick of potato and grease in a styrofoam container on the floor, by the bed where I'd slept cinched between Megan and Skobie. So Konrad came in when I was half-sitting, propped on elbows and trying to peel the brick apart with a plastic fork that kept bending from the thickness of it.

Konrad and Arron were going to Ottawa for four days, so I got up to hug them, Goodbye, and good riddance, have fun and say hi to everyone, et cetera —

They were going to convocation, receiving their prestigious university degrees: Arron in architecture and Konrad in civil engineering — and they would miss three days of planting and go on a holiday into the real world. They would see their families, shave their faces, and shake black leathery hands with academics. Of course, it was my convocation, too, but I didn't attend because I thought maybe I should plant trees and make money, and I thought that probably convocation would be pretty boring and maybe I had better things to do.

In the end I might as well have gone to Ottawa to see my friends, because after just one day of planting on Day 29, Tom stood up to tell us we'd be frozen for a while.

18

The day was a roller coaster, anyway. Day 29 I woke up with my head thick, nose clogged and lungs full of phlegm. Eyes puffy and everything pounding with the virus or whatever it was. Tendonitis in both elbows — that familiar old creak — and a cold grey morning somewhat miserable, damp and hungover.

Buldyke took over our crew for the day since Konrad was gone. Buldyke was a six-year veteran and the most experienced planter in the camp. In other camps, of course, there might have been ten-year, twenty-year veterans — but that would generally be out west, BC. Our camp, Ontario, was full of students, rookies, kids.

So Buldyke was the most experienced, and he ran the crew. That morning he gifted me with a nice slice of land, sandy and straight, because we'd planted together two years prior; we had that bond of being ol' vets reunited in a half-rookie camp.

Make a lot of money, he said, Just kill it today, You got straight sandy furrows in there.

Straight sandy furrows: every planter's dream.

Okay, okay, I tried, but things started off badly because I'd forgotten my music in my tent, and, well, I really loved to hear music all day — I mean, it seemed to make all of the difference in the world to me, back then,

But this day would be a quiet one, suffocatingly quiet —

Okay, okay, but I needed to focus on these straight sandy furrows.

I started off with a rummage through three slimy bundles of moldy jack pine — because, of course, jack pine wants to be planted in sand, and by the looks of it, there was sand —

But, then when I charged down the first little hillside, there was no sand, and there was swamp instead. Black mirror-coloured swamp and bristling grass — and, of course, you can't plant jack pine in a swamp, because jack pine wants sand — so that set me back to begin with — and then I paused, and paused for a second — and then I wasn't moving fast enough —

— I wasn't moving fast enough —

Day 29: that was when my shovel broke and started clinking. Something inside of the hollow steel shaft came loose, some little metal nut, so that every time I stabbed the ground my shovel went like:

shckt

That's what it kept saying to me — every six seconds, or so:

shckt

And meanwhile, lungs heavy with phlegm, and orange brain fluid leaking from one nostril

shckt

Cranky elbows and that old splintering shin

shckt

And now I was mad because I couldn't plant pine in the swamp and I had to go splashing across

shckt

Not planting any trees

shckt

Wasting time, wasting time, I'm not moving fast enough

shckt

And I'm not moving fast enough and now where's the furrow gone

shckt

And the buzzing of deerflies and the heaviness of ten more hours

shckt

I'm not moving fast enough

shckt

Not moving fast enough and only ten more hours

shkct

Not moving fast enough and —

shkct

It was Mandog who said, as a rookie, what he learned:

shckt

That you can't change the volume of the voice inside your head.

shckt

And me, I tried to change the volume because I wanted it to shut the fuck up,

shckt

And what I found was this:

shckt

It's not nice to hear your internal monologue as though it's yelling in your ears —

shckt

But it's even worse to hear your internal monologue

shckt

In a stream of frantic whispering

shckt

When you're alone for ten hours —

shckt

Don't let your mind start whispering to you

shckt

Because that's gotta be what drives people crazy.

shckt

And I wasn't moving fast enough,

shckt

And not only that,

shckt

But I really wanted my shovel to shut the fuck up, too.

shckt

And that's probably when I started talking to myself.

I didn't have much to say; it was just ten words.

I repeated one sentence to myself, ten words, first in my mind — normal volume, not whispering. I zeroed in on the words to block out the sound of the shovel in my ears, so that there was nothing but one sentence on repeat inside of my brain, and then I started thinking faster and louder, and the words came out in my breath, panting fast-planting breaths, sentences running in circles and grabbing each other by the tail—

The day passed by and all I did was say the same ten words to myself on repeat, as quickly and as frantically as those ten words could possibly be spoken, for eight, nine hours. And at some point I arrived at an empty state of bliss and everything around opened up into this suspended instant of delirious rhythmic beauty, and I did nothing else all day, just kept saying the same ten words over and over and over again, and I planted trees, and I made some good money.

19

When Tom gave us the news that night about the frozen trees, no one got angry.

Mostly, that's because it was Tom, and that's how it was with him. No one could be angry with Tom because he was experienced and competent while also being completely understated. He was the camp supervisor, and he was the leader, certainly — but for many he was foremost a friend.

Here are the things I know about Tom:

That year was his tenth season in the bush. He'd planted for six years and crew-bossed for three.

In the off-season he'd been a student for just as long.

He'd studied journalism, history, geography, and natural resource management.

He'd spent two or more years traveling, and had no plan for his life.

He had a girlfriend who was a platinum grade ex-bush-veteran. She had planted over one million trees in her career, and she was hard as fuck.

Tom looked good. He was a scruffy Tom Cruise cast halfway between a country lad and a pirate. When he spoke to the planter girls, they swooned. (Should I say we?)

He didn't actually speak that much. When he did, it was generally in the form of dry witty humour, with a tendency to be oddly elaborate.

And as far as anyone could tell, the only things Tom cared about were sports teams, country music, and beer.

Beer:

That's how he pacified everyone after announcing that the tree nursery had Fucked Us, Yet Again.

Tom tried to secure some compensation for us, for the work and the money that was lost. Which was an unprecedented thing, already — because in general, as tree planters, we learned not to expect compensation when things went wrong.

But Tom applied to his own supervisor, the Company's Operations Manager, for some funding. And this is what he offered us:

While we were stuck idly in the bush, we wouldn't have to pay Camp Cost; we would eat for free. Furthermore, the Company would fund a day's worth of leisure activities in town so that we wouldn't really be stuck idly in the bush at all. And furthermore, the Company was buying us a few rounds of beer.

There was a liability issue there, apparently: no one was allowed to get drunk and stupid on Company money — so

Tom was only allowed to provide a drink or two per person, and not enough to get anyone drunk.

So, said Tom, There's enough beer in the back of my truck for everyone to have about six — Not enough to get anyone drunk.

So there was laughter and applause about that, and no one could really be angry.

We spent the night drinking in camp. It was a mild night, of course, because it really took a few days of work before everyone could get built up into an orgiastic frenzy. And the next day we rolled to town to spend the day drinking at the bowling alley, which was apparently the only leisure space that would take us.

But there was that restlessness, you know — there was something that took hold and made our wheels spin like crazy, like a car revving in neutral until we were back at work. Tom gave us the news again, the following night, Day 30: we were still watching the ice melt. Yet another Day Off, another day of waiting.

So that was the first day, Day 31, that I spent working with Yukon as a volunteer, mostly out of restlessness and also because we hadn't had much time to hang out, lately.

20

The tree deliverers — Yukon, Parks, and Bennett — worked every day, and often enough they started early and finished late. Yukon worked for seventy-six days straight; zero days off.

The deliverers spent the days moving trees. They had to ensure that the seedlings were on the block and ready to be planted, every day all day, so that the planters could always be working, always with unbridled urgency.

During this particular season, the trees continued to arrive in mostly-frozen reefers for the entirety of the contract, which added an extra step to the deliverers' process: they had to rotate loads of bundles, out of the reefers and into the sun to thaw, and then onto the blocks and spread out at caches — and the trees had to be thawed, but not too thawed because they weren't allowed to get dried out — and if they were dry or if they were frozen everyone would get in trouble from the Client.

So on Day 31 we moved trees. I rode in the passenger seat of Yukon's F150 and we hauled bundles around. Out of the reefer and into the sun, then onto the truck and then under the tarps, spread out around the block for the planters. Empty caches cleaned up, half-empty caches restocked, and so on.

A cache was nothing but a pile of trees underneath a tarp. The deliverers would put the caches wherever they saw fit to do so. There was nothing pre-established along the logging roads; until we arrived, there was nothing but endless spreads of clearcut on either side of some narrow gravel track — if there was even that.

Yukon and I were working with Parks, that day, to prepare a block for Gabe's crew. There was this mud pit across the road, at the entrance to the block — a massive flooded sinkhole. We watched Parks drive through and we saw his truck go pitching wildly to one side and the wheels go sliding under — then slowly he came up on the other side. We followed, careful, and everything on the dashboard — insurance papers, block maps, cigarettes — went flying while the mud rocked the truck like waves and we went airborne against our seatbelts.

So later in the day, while we were dropping tree-loads along the deeply muddy track between the clearcuts, Parks tried to find another way out. He went exploring out the back end of the block, looking for an easier road so that the van could drive in the next day, so that the crew wouldn't have to walk. Then when he radioed Yukon to say that he was stuck in the mud, Yukon held the radio in his hand without pressing the speak-button and looked at me, rolled his eyes annoyed: Rookie Mistake, he said, What a dumbass.

We met Parks with his wheels just semicircles above the mud and Yukon said: You shouldn't have done that —

And that was the extent of the conversation. I was watching like a tourist as they hitched the trucks and backed up, and Parks came spinning out of the mud swerving backwards.

When I climbed back into the passenger seat, Yukon was silent for a minute. Then he looked over at me, cocked his head and said, Hey, I'm sorry for being grumpy,

And he said, Really it wasn't Parks' fault since the F250 is heavier than the F150, And the road is shit — And, sorry, And I'm not going to be angry about it anymore.

And I just grinned at that, raised my eyebrows. Okay, I said — because he'd hardly been angry in the first place.

And the F250 got stuck again, on the way out where the mud was like cake batter, and this time Yukon didn't say anything, just hitched up the tow hooks and pulled him out.

We finished work, the three of us together, packing garbage and skids and aspenite boards back into the empty reefer to send back to the nursery. Two days had gone by, then, and the trees we'd laid out were thawed, so we'd be able to work again the next day, and everyone was relieved about that.

So the next day we moved into the burn blocks and ripped open the sun-thawed bundles of jack pine, and hey — what do you know — they were still moldy.

21

When we rolled home after work on Day 31, the rest of the camp was there playing baseball, riding out the final idle day. I watched the game while sitting on Yukon's tailgate and I had a beer and a smoke with Stefan. That was when Arron and Konrad came back from our convocation in Ottawa, so I had a beer and a smoke with Arron, too, and I was truly happy to see him.

The rest of that night was like any night, then, with the sky getting reddish and the gravel floor getting textured in shadow. Like any night when the silence of dusk crept over us, and then there were only the sounds of the wind and the rumble of the generator, maybe broken by a truck rolling in — maybe Tom working late. And sporadically, there was the angry staccato of planters coughing through the night — that phlegmy hacking that would bounce across the campsite like an argument —

Hack-hack, floating thinly out of one anonymous tent, and then an answer, hack-hack-hack from across the plateau, and maybe a third, or a fourth, or all night long. This violent chorus of illness, it was just a lullaby, another thing so easy to ignore. Same as the way we ignored it whenever someone paused mid-conversation to shoot clods of snot out of each nostril, one at a time — though later in the real world I had to make a forced effort to correct that habit.

Nighttime routine: almost always the same, down to the details. After dinner I would stand and brush my teeth with Stefan, or Megan, or Arron, beside the blue plastic water barrels propped horizontal on steel cages. Stand and grin and shoot out conversation, and shoot out toothpaste into the gravel and kick at the tiny rocks to kill the white stains of it. I would fill my aluminum canteen with cold water from the barrels, every night, and bring it to bed. Sometime after midnight I'd reach out and find it, invisible in the dark but obvious by habit, and I would drink three-quarters of it then. In the mornings, the one-quarter remainder was important, because I would fill it again with boiling water from the breakfast table, and the aluminum would burn my hands unless I left a little buffer in it.

Same habits every night, every morning — I learned exactly how much cold water to leave in the canteen so that it would warm my hands, every morning, and not burn them. I would drink plain hot water with breakfast, and I got so used to it that even from a faucet, I still draw it hot.

Day 32: after two days of rest, we slipped smoothly back into routine.

Day 32: I was hunched over a plastic table against the plastic wall of the mess tent with both hands clasped tight around my almost-but-not-quite-boiling canteen. Eyes half-closed, always, breathing through my mouth because of that leaking brain fluid always clogging the rest, and felt that hackingness come clawing up my throat so I coughed, hack-hack-hack, wetly like everyone.

And that's when one of the rookie girls walked by and looked at me and said,

You have mold in your lungs,

And I said, No, it's just bronchitis or something.

I heard you coughing, she said, We all have the same thing, We all have mold in our lungs.

Aw, I said, Fuck that, and I frowned at the thought of it. Then Mandog leaned over from where he was sitting and he said:

Imagine what it looks like, Everyone's lungs are full of cobwebs.

Just like the trees.

Fuck that, I said.

And I stood, creakily, to move out for morning meeting — same routine — to throw my six-litre water-bag on the roof with my planting bags and shovel, to sit and listen to Tom and brush my teeth into the gravel and lace my boots and wrap them in duct tape and load into the van and go back to sleep for an hour,

So I didn't think about it anymore, then,

But I thought about it later: later in the day, while I was bent over my shovel, sandwiched between the bare mid-day sun and the bony charred ash of the ground, and I was coughing and spitting, head pounding and stomach revolting — I thought of it then —

Moldy lungs. Of course.

I coughed harder. Wanted to see cobwebs splattering out onto the ground.

We were planting the jack pine that day, jack pine for the dry ashy burn-land, and it was all thawed now, but yes it was half limp-grey with cobwebby mold, same as before. We were still sorting through it, ten times a day, digging with our fingers through the slime and making piles of corpses on the roadsides.

We rummaged, we dumped, we tossed limp handfuls into piles, and faster, and faster, filled our bags and we went marching in, and coughing and spitting and planting furiously, faster-harder-faster and we practiced our hard-earned numbness and kept our eyes half-open on the ground.

22

When I first met Yukon and Stefan, I met them at the same time, and I couldn't tell them apart. They were always to-gether, and both of them very tall and lean, with blonde hair that was neither short nor long, and they were quiet enough that it took a while to get to know them. Always as a pair, they were drifting around the fringes of the action, and always half-smiling half-joking half-sarcastic, like they'd both be profoundly cynical if they weren't so perfectly amused.

I met them in my first season of tree planting — back when I was a hapless wide-eyed rookie — and I didn't really speak to either of them until that contract was already over. By then, of course, I'd realized that they didn't really look much alike. Though they were close like brothers they weren't actually related.

Yukon was light, light in colour and in gait, narrow and tense with a gravelly smoker's voice and sharp blue eyes like ice. I thought he was probably crazy, in his way; crazy in his intensity.

Stefan, slightly less so. He was earthier — more powerfully built but more softly mannered. We talked about art together; Stefan was a sculptor. He would talk with this low voice so deep I could barely hear it — and if I leaned in to listen, what struck me was: Shit, This guy is hilarious.

Those were my impressions of Yukon and Stefan, when I was a rookie. Again, by the time I really knew them we'd already planted together for two months. By then, the spring contract in Northern Ontario was drawing to a close, and I didn't really have any plans after that, and then somehow we all wound up together.

That was the very end of June, and we would have been camped at the Campground then — the final site, every year — but the Campground was on fire that season. Instead we were parked at this hilly glade inside a dark poplar forest, where the ground was always popping with fireworks of grasshoppers, and where we were beset by plague of black bears for the final two weeks.

The bears first arrived while we were in town for a Day Off. We came home to a mess: garbage and garbage cans scattered, and a handful of tents ripped and ravaged. Then it kept happening. As the saying goes, A Fed Bear is a Dead Bear, because once a bear finds food it won't back off until you shoot it — but we didn't have the authority to shoot, so we just waited out the rest of the contract while living in this oscillating harmony with the shy sharp-clawed beasts. Every day when we came home from work there would be just a little more damage done — another tent or two reduced to ponds of fabric in the grass, and the garbage everywhere, and everything in the mess tent shredded up. The bears feasted on anything — food, yes, also plastic containers, dry protein powder, deodorant and toothpaste, beer and motor oil.

There were two bears. At night we would hear them snuffling around in the bushes, shuffling between the tents. Almost nightly we were woken by the territorial barking of the camp dogs as they chased the pests, or by the smashing of pot lids together, blanks being fired, and the theatrical shouting of one insomnia-plagued crew boss who seemed to enjoy the standoff.

When a tent was bulldozed by a bear during the workday, its owner would sigh and pack up and move in with a friend. There was only a week or two left, anyway.

My tent wasn't targeted by the bears but I did move in with Arron for the final three nights of work, since my floor leaked during a storm and all my blankets got sodden. I abandoned ship and slept with Arron and discovered that Arron's tent was immeasurably more comfortable than my own, which was probably because I'd just spent two months sleeping on a thick sheet of bubble wrap. The bubble wrap, I think, was the reason that I would wake up in the night whimpering aloud while my lower back was paralyzed with cramping, and it would take me a solid minute to roll onto one side and make it stop.

When that Ontario contract was over I was enjoying it so much that I signed up for the next one.

The next contract, spanning the month of July, was going to take place near Fredericton in New Brunswick, but there was still a week left before it would start; a week to kill before we had anywhere to be. So on the very last day in Northern Ontario, even as we were tearing down camp for the last time, I was trying to figure out where I was going to sleep the following night.

I was thinking about that while sweeping out the Virgin Mary's school bus — or at least, while making a show of sweeping the bus in order to escape the hard labour jobs — and Yukon was there, likely enough avoiding the teardown as well. He was a second-year planter, then, not yet a deliverer, and he was just lounging in the driver's seat of the bus when I said to him,

Hey, do you want to go to Ottawa?

Which was a strange thing, because we really weren't friends, but it had just occurred to me that Ottawa was en route to Fredericton, and I had an empty student house there, guzzling rent over the summer,

And it had just occurred to me that if everyone went to Ottawa for a week, then all of this mania and all this mad momentum — all of it could just carry on, as long as everyone stuck together — it could be Day Off for a week —

So I invited Yukon and I was surprised when he said, Yeah Okay.

He and Stefan were both from the west coast, near Vancouver, so they had nowhere to be, either. They weren't about to fly home for the week, and neither of them had really seen Ottawa, and Yukon said, Sure, We can be like tourists, Why not?

So that's how it went. In the end maybe twelve of us spent the week around the capital city, waiting on the Company convoy to drive us out to New Brunswick. But it was only four of us who spent the week camped out in my living room, spent the week glued together at the hips and unexpectedly unearthing a solid friendship in the midst of a long alcoholic binge.

§ § § § §

Two years after that, the subject of the Ottawa Week came up in conversation between Yukon and I. The first time we talked about it, we were drunk at the bonfire and it was 3 am and he said to me, That was one of the best weeks of my life.

The second time we spoke of it, we were sober, delivering frozen blocks of trees on Day 31, and that time he said this:

A lot has changed since then; nowadays none of us would drink the swish.

The swish was this four-month-old keg beer we'd found in the pantry at my student house: a 59-litre keg still half full. The beer was cloudy and warm, and it was perfectly flat and tasted like vinegar, and the four of us pulled the keg into the living room beside the couches and sat down and drank it, day in and day out so that the days turned cloudy like the swish, and someone decided that the Swish Challenge was to finish the whole keg before we left, and I can't remember whether or not we ever did, but we certainly made a good attempt of it.

So when Yukon said, Nowadays none of us would drink the swish,

I laughed and said —

I don't know about that, Maybe I still would.

But he was right: a lot of things had changed since then, and Ben — Ben the camp highballer, who'd been the fourth member of our Ottawa crew during that bender of sunny afternoons and blurry dawns — Ben just said that he'd grown up since then. So it was funny that two years later the four of us were still working in the same camp in Northern Ontario and we were still doing the same thing all day, every day, like nothing had changed — but in the end, I guess, things change and people do too.

23

Ben was a rookie the same year that I was. He was on the same crew as Arron and Konrad, while I was on Amo's all-rookie crew. Ben and I really met each other by being outrageously drunk all the time, both of us and equally, and I guess that's why we got along so well. We wound up together, in those mornings when the night should have been over, wound up climbing out of hotel windows to watch the white-pink sunrises on the waves of rooftops below. The hotel became a playground in the light of dawn, and everything was an adventure.

As rookies we rode the elevator up and down, for how many hours, lying half-horizontal on the floor, until the door opened and a man with a briefcase told us he was going to work and told us we should probably leave—and we had to scoop up all our empty blue cans by the armful, and we had to wheel Ben's crew boss back to his room on a luggage cart. On another occasion we hid from the police behind a vending machine, because of some noise complaint, and I could barely stop laughing long enough to get away with it. We once found a laundry room hidden behind a closed door and we felt like we'd stumbled upon the New World, and we missed the sunrise that morning because we spent the wee hours seated reverently at the foot of the laundry machines in that secret windowless room.

Everything was new, then. No matter what happened, it was a great adventure. We'd never been tree planters before.

In Fredericton Ben and I were on the same crew. We worked together, often. He was always a faster planter and he taught me things—Keep your back low, he said, Focus on one thing at a time. On the van rides we slept on each other, every day, back and forth. We massaged each other's aching shoulders with shiny blackstained hands. We camped side-by-side and I could hear him coughing through the night — Planter's Cough: I don't what it means but I know what it sounds like.

That month in Fredericton — still my first season planting trees —

That month blends together for me, all blends into one gorgeous sunny afternoon — endless, wild and warm. East-coast July. Days spent low-backed under the blue sky, evenings spent splashing through the shallow river behind the campsite, where we would wade in and duck down, hold onto a rock and let the current stretch us weightless. Our campsite, that month, was so close to civilization that I could see someone's backyard from my tent.

In my memory, only one day of rain. It was black swamp ground under a grey sky and rainwater like needles on our skin. Floating out of the air that day I heard these bouts of agonized screaming, echoing eerily over the empty land. I had no idea what I was hearing, and wondered as I worked.

Ben hadn't been the one screaming, but he told me what the screaming was about, when we met at the roadside and his face was dark and blank and he told me,

I just got stung by twelve hornets and my legs are going numb,

And then he bagged up more trees without pausing to kneel and he went back into his land, faster than I did.

There were more days of rain — oh, certainly — but that's the only one I remember. The rest of it was sun, dry dust on the teeth, smiles and thick dark skin, freedom and the sense of being invincible.

Sunny days and starry nights, a bunch of drunk kids feeling good —

Same as the week we spent in Ottawa, when Yukon and I stayed awake until 9 am beside the keg of swish, every night, every morning, just Talking Shit, he said. Yukon talked about glory — I'm only in it for the glory, he said — and he's been saying it ever since. And it's almost sarcastic, you know, but it isn't. We'd wake up in the afternoons and eat poutine for every meal, drinking and smoking and up every night through the dawn, with our gear and our dirt and our keg sprawled out all over the living room floor and all of us rotating, beds, couches, floorspace, didn't matter.

We were getting excited about tree planting again, talking about tree planting, just a few days left, and off to Fredericton! All together! We were going out into the yard and ripping up the lawn with our shovels and talking about planting trees, until the stars faded and the sky was going pink again and Ben and I were asleep, together, spooning in the dewy grass — and together as we drove across the country for two days, two days spent sleeping off the hangover, lying across each other on the seat — and together in our tents side-by-side between the trees, and in the vans, and in the clearcuts, and later in the logging camp, and after that driving all the way back across the country, another two days — still together.

And Ben and I were the only ones left of our entire camp when we reached the Greyhound station in Toronto, parted ways with a quick hug and no eye contact, and that was the end of that.

I didn't see any of them for two years and then when we talked about it again Yukon just told me,

Things have changed since then,

And I laughed but he was right.

Things change, yeah. A little bit less excitable, now, and a little bit less invincible, too.

24

Pretty soon after my first season of tree planting, I broke my leg in half.

It was my left leg and it snapped completely. Two bones, tibia and fibula, maybe fifteen centimetres above the ankle. I was lucky.

I was back in school when that happened, back in Ottawa, just after my rookie season. By then the mad highs and lows of the summer had leveled out again — back to the regular buzzing grind of the real world. It was the first day of October, and I will always remember that. I will always remember that it was the same day that my sister moved to South Korea — and she was gone alone and out of touch, and it occurred to her while she was flying that someone in Canada might have died and she wouldn't even know about it — and eventually she found out that no one had died, but the verdict was that I'd gotten pretty close.

It was nine in the morning and I was in the workshop at school, doing work, folding metal.

One person witnessed this whole thing, and that was my friend and fellow student Gabby. It started with Gabby telling me that she couldn't find any half-inch plywood. The plywood wasn't in its regular storage shelf because the shop was overstocked.

I was aware of this because I spent a lot of time there; I was also aware that the wood was temporarily being stored in the welding room, so I brought Gabby there. We found the half-inch plywood standing in a stack of four-by-eight-foot sheets, leaning against the wall. In front of it, there was a stack of one-inch plywood, also standing, leaning on top, making the half-inch inaccessible.

So I pulled the stack of one-inch plywood upright, thinking that if Gabby stood at one edge she could slide a piece of half-inch out from behind it. As it turned out, this was a bad idea because the stack of one-inch plywood weighed about eight hundred pounds. They made that calculation after it landed on me.

The stack of wood was almost a foot thick. The first time I tried to pull it away from the wall, it didn't budge. So I pulled hard — I mean, I really yanked on it — and it came upright, and then it was vertical, and then — of course — I couldn't actually stop it.

Time pauses in moments like that: when you know that you've really fucked up, just a split-second too late.

One step behind me, a heavy steel welding table was bolted to the floor, with a single sheet of wood leaning against it like a wall at my back.

One step in front of me, eight hundred pounds of wood, tipping fast.

I stepped back — one step back — and I pushed against the falling wood, both palms and all of my force — both palms against the top edge, chest high —

And that's when I had that time-stopping, heart-stopping moment of realizing that something bad was about to happen —

I mean, something really, really bad —

Something like a contest of strength between this unstoppable falling thing — momentum and gravity and eight hundred pounds — and a frail human ribcage, heart and lungs and spine —

And then somehow I got kind of lucky, because somehow it was only my leg. I stepped back and I pushed on the wood, and that's when my leg snapped in half.

The snap was audible. In my memory it was like a gunshot, and then my leg wasn't holding me up anymore and I was just hanging, both hands still pressed against the stack of wood, with the stack of wood pressed against my sternum, pinning me in place.

My heart was pounding in my ears and everything was spinning. Gabby was staring at me with her mouth open and she was frozen, and I said to her,

I think I just broke my leg.

She stared at me and didn't move, didn't move at all, and I really wanted her to move, because things were really bad.

I enunciated at her, carefully:

This is *really bad*.

That's when another student walked into the tight little space, came strolling through the doors whistling. He came in and stopped abruptly, and did a triple-take between Gabby and I, back and forth with his head, almost laughable. He tells me — and I don't remember this, personally — he tells me that I looked at him and said very calmly,

I'm dying.

Then he grabbed at the wood and tried to lift it, and couldn't, and he ran and got some help, and the two of them lifted the wood, a few pieces at a time, and I slid down to the floor and sat there with my legs bent behind me and I looked at my hands spread out on the ground with everything spinning, blackish, and my heart like a jackhammer.

One of the guys told me that I had to move, then. Some of the wood was still hovering above me.

You have to move, they said, We can't take this wood away, There isn't enough space, You have to get out from under it.

I *can't*. My leg is *broken*.

But I had to, so I moved, hands first, legs sliding behind, and there was the chilling sensation of the left foot dangling sideways and sickeningly dragging along.

When I was out from under the wood I sat still and looked at the floor and breathed very deeply and played with the dust under my fingers, and I never looked back at my leg because I didn't want to see what it looked like.

25

I looked at it later, when I was in a hospital bed, later that day, when they took off the temporary splint and they man-handled my bones back into place. That was the most painful moment of my life, because by then the shock had worn off, and it was just these raw waves of pain, overwhelming pow-erful raw pain. The shock had made me feel drunk at first — I remember saying that out loud, while the paramedics were surrounding me in the welding room: I feel like I'm *way too drunk* right now — that's what I said — and after a little while I kind of had to laugh even though it hurt so much — I mean, it hurt more than anything, but I didn't know what else to do except focus on breathing, and breathing so hard that the paramedics asked if I was having trouble breathing — and they double-checked my spine and ribs, maybe six times, and I said, No, Sorry, I'm just breathing really loudly, Sorry, It's really just my leg — and they said, You don't have to apolo-gize — but I did, and I aplogized to the workshop people, too, for breaking my leg in their workshop, and I really felt bad about it, because I felt pretty stupid in the end — and fuck, fuck, it hurt, and I swore a lot, too.

But this also happened:

Before I even went to the hospital, I was still in the work-shop, laid out on a stretcher, and my roommate came to see me and we started joking around and she said to me:

Which is worse, this or tree planting?

And, at that point, I still hadn't had my bones aligned properly — they were still in four pieces — and everything felt totally obscene, and still I answered her — honestly, I said:

Tree planting was worse than this.

When I finally looked at my leg, in the hospital, it was just a bloody mess. I really couldn't see anything. The bone had ripped right out of my leg and it was just like a little flower made of blood and flesh and skin, erupting from the shin, and it never really healed right so I could always feel it after that.

It was five weeks until I could walk again, and then only carefully. I didn't have a cast on my leg: instead, a surgeon drilled a hole into the tibia, just under the knee, and inserted a 35-centimetre-long titanium tube inside of the bone to line up the broken pieces. He screwed the tube into place with one screw at the ankle and two below the knee. The smaller bone, the fibula, was left to heal on its own.

The day after surgery, my roommates visited me in the hospital and we discussed the accident ad nauseam. We went through it again and again, dissecting every gruesome detail until Darby stood up and left the room saying that she was about to throw up.

My shin-bone ripped a hole in my jeans, I said,

And Darby left the room. The rest of us kept going over it —

So the stack of wood must have hit your leg.

No, it didn't.

But then, how . . .

Nothing hit my leg — The wood hit my chest. See, there's scratches under my collarbone where the edge of the plywood scraped down — And how could a flat piece of wood have hit my collarbone and my leg at the same time, when my leg was behind me? Nothing hit that leg —

And what about the falling plywood? Why did the plywood stop falling?

Well, the edge of the wood caught the corner of the welding table — so some of the weight was taken off there, so then when it landed on my chest I was able to hold it off with my arms —

So then — Then imagine, if it hadn't hit the welding table first — Then, Holy shit —

Then it would have been a lot worse.

Like —

Yeah, a lot worse.

Like, what if you were actually dead right now?

. . . Yeah.

And I don't know whether this is something that we worked out together, my three roommates and I — Maybe —

But I have a feeling that it's something I worked out on my own while replaying that incident a thousand times over in my memory, a thousand times over at least —

That I slid down under that wood because my leg gave out — That if I'd been standing up straight, those eight hundred pounds would have hit my rib cage, would have landed against my spine, long before they landed on the corner of that welding table. But instead, two other bones snapped in half, snapped right in the middle of my shin for some reason —

My left leg gave out of its own accord and the rest of me just slipped underneath, and just barely.

So as I said, I was lucky.

When they found out about it, my parents each said they would drive up to Ottawa and look after me, at least for the long weekend, and I said no.

No, I said. Just No.

Over the phone at least twice I said, Do not drive to Ottawa.

It's not even a big deal, I said, People break bones all the time.

And what was that all about?

That vehement decision to lie in bed alone and explore the effects of synthetic morphine, while all of my roommates left the city to spend Thanksgiving weekend with their families?

Something about not wanting to go through those details again. Something about not wanting to break down over it, and also not wanting to break it down —

Not wanting to acknowledge the fact that, sure, maybe people break bones all the time, but maybe not always like that.

26

Then life goes on, and life goes fast. That autumn I finished the rest of my semester at school. I took ten days off to get stoned in bed, and then after ten days I went back.

I stayed awake for one full night to catch up on what I'd missed. I sat up on the couch where Yukon and I had once sat up drinking swish through the dawns, and I propped my leg up on a pillow and it sat up there pounding bright red and full of staples. I downed a thousand cups of instant coffee and threw some work together and was still awake in a zombie-like state for a presentation at ten the next morning, which I attended on crutches with my entire body throbbing from the swelling in my leg.

Also I was furious the entire time. And after a month or two I was ready to drop out of school again.

The rest of the fall, I stumbled my way along. Morphine was for sleeping and caffeine was for staying awake. My roommates were generous with me and they drove me to school and back, sometimes to the grocery store, and I never went anywhere else.

Sometime in that interval, a bunch of tree planters drove up to Ottawa to blow a weekend away — I don't remember who exactly; Gabe was there, Maddie — and Ben. I wanted to see Ben, and they told me to meet them at a club downtown. I couldn't walk well enough to go to a club, and Ben didn't have a phone, and we never met up, and truly I never saw anyone outside of school for three full months, and things were pretty low. And all the time — if I let my mind go there — I could still feel the force of eight hundred pounds hitting me square in the chest.

27

I was ready to drop out of school again, and the only reason I stuck around was so that I could move to France. This semester abroad had been dangling in front of me like bait — so I held out, survived the autumn, snatched up that bait and escaped to Paris.

It was February, then, and I was able to walk without limping. And it was a relief to be on the move, and those months in Paris were good.

On the other hand, leaving Canada meant an abrupt end to my physiotherapy, and my leg kept reminding me it was there, still sharp and always aching.

That semester in France lasted through June, and I missed the entire tree planting contract in Ontario. At the end of the semester, I flew back to Canada. I was broke and I was in need of work.

I called the Company and invited myself to Fredericton, but the Fredericton contract was already full and they didn't need any more planters there.

But, they said, There is an opening in Manitoba.

And I needed money — quick money — and what else was I going to do? There were a bunch of reasons that I went back, and I don't regret it, but that was a really tough month, that July.

I went back to make a few thousand bucks, yes — and also because I missed the feeling of it, the invincibility, the insanity of it — and because I'd never quite mastered the art of tree planting, and I just wasn't done with it yet. On another level, I also wanted my left leg back; still it was shaky, still it was weak, and the doctors said it wouldn't hurt — I mean, they said it wouldn't get any worse, even if it hurt.

I flew to Toronto from Paris, and then, exactly one week later — on Canada Day, exactly nine months after my leg snapped underneath me — I flew to Winnipeg and took a bus eight hours northwest to The Pas, Manitoba, and I started planting trees.

When I arrived at the camp, there were about thirty people working there. By the end, eight of those people remained. Planters — and a crew boss — dropped off one by one, as the conditions and the camp morale plummeted in sync. I was one of four females in the camp; my crew was entirely young rookie men, and by the end of it my crew was gone.

There was a saying in this camp, a single phrase that kept running around in circles, always floating in the air with the bugs and the rain. The saying originated with the veterans, and the rookies had taken it up like a mantra. If anything happened, if anyone complained, everyone had one response:

Well, that's tree plantin' for ya.

It was the answer to everything — You asked for it, didn't you? Didn't you know what you were getting into?

If not — Well, that's tree plantin' for ya.

It was a record season for bugs. Mosquitoes were the worst.

After dinner and breakfast, as it goes, we were supposed to wash our dishes in the plastic hose-sink behind the cook shack. The mosquitoes were so ferocious around the sink that some of the planters ceased to wash their dishes entirely; instead they let the dogs lick them clean, and then ate off them again without ever going near the sinks. We got used to eating with hoods on, everything covered up except the fingers and the face, got used to blowing mosquitoes off our lips and cheeks, got used to swallowing an insect or two with every bite, and after dinner we immediately took refuge in our tents, alone. There was no reason to stay awake.

Perhaps the highlight of the whole contract was the helicopter rides. Tiny flying machines, human-scale insects, so light that we could feel the sensations of flight. The pilot would do dips and turns for the hell of it and we would all whoop for more, calling giddily into the blocky headsets. Manitoba below us: a green shag carpet stretched flat between horizons, broken sometimes by dark blue water and more often by little brown-bristle patches of clearcut. We'd dip down and hustle out and plant in groups of four, incredibly isolated together between the black walls of swamp trees, walls of black spruce unbroken in any direction.

The helicopter work only lasted four days. For the rest of it, we walked in. The blocks were too remote — inaccessible by road. We walked a lot. An hour or two, into the block, an hour or two, out of the block. Unpaid walking, heads down into the rain, wet feet, wet pants, wet everything, and there were so many bugs that it felt like we were walking through layers of bloodsucking cobwebs. Clouds of carnivores, clouds of rain, dark endless clouds. Heads down, walk. Ignore.

That's tree plantin' for ya.

The planters in this camp had red bubbling wounds on their shoulders, backs and ribcages. They had branded each other with a piece of wire twisted into the shape of a spruce tree, wire heated up in a campfire. The scars didn't heal into the shape of a spruce tree. They popped and blistered, chafing, infected, and healed up twisted and malformed.

They asked me if I wanted one.

You guys are fucked, I told them.

Towards the end, enough of the rookies had given up and left. Another whole camp was called in, to help us finish the trees.

The arriving camp came in from a few towns over. They told us that they'd had a fifteen-kilometre walk into work one day, into a block that they called Vimy Ridge. A four-hour trudge before the workday began — carrying everything on their backs and fighting against ankle-deep mud — four hours walking, unpaid. Then a little while after that, it had happened again: another walk-in that seemed endless, though in reality it was shorter than the first. It wasn't quite fifteen kilometres, the second time around — but the memory of the previous ordeal was enough to make some of the planters give up, throw in the towel and refuse to work. In response the supervisor brought in a Rolligon: an all-terrain vehicle with tires the height of a human being. Then instead of the long trudge in, the planters huddled together in the back of the Rolligon while the vehicle made its way through the mud at a pace that was slower than walking. Something like two hours to get into the block, and two hours to get back out: they huddled on the open-air platform with a tarp on top of their heads, and the clouds pissed rain on them the entire time.

Well, we told them, That's tree plantin' for ya.

The contract was more than halfway done by the time I arrived there. I ate dinner with the camp's veterans every day — the few, hard veterans: five years, six years, fifteen years under their belts. They had nothing to say about it except, Well, That's tree plantin' for ya — and I didn't have much to say either.

I spent the days walking, as we all did. Fifty extra pounds to carry — trees, gear, water, whatever it was — and one leg shaky and twisted and shooting pain like bullets.

My leg was stronger by the end of it. By the end of it, it was sore — god, it was fucking sore — but it was balanced again. The work had been physiotherapy, in a way. Masochistic twelve-hour days of sudden rehabilitation — and by the end I'd remembered my balance; both legs had evened out.

In the end, that's how it always seemed to go. Everything evens out: you get used to it.

You can get used to anything, if you want to. And maybe you wind up just a little bit numb and a little bit hard, but you're fine either way. That's tree planting for you.

At the end of July, the trees were gone and the season was over, and that was fine by me. We went west and got drunk, and I went further west than the rest of them, stayed drunk more or less for another three weeks, and then I went back to school.

That was my second season of tree planting; it lasted just under a month, and I only worked for nineteen days.

28

In my third season we were at the Campground for forty-five days, which was the longest I'd ever camped in one place. We moved there on Day 27 and stayed until Day 72.

The Campground was a wide flat clearing surrounded by burnt forest. On one side there was a swampy little pond and on the other side, beyond the rows of the black-char matchstick tree trunks, there was the highway. Across the highway was the real campground, with a beach and a lake and a bunch of sedentary people in RV's. On good days we would go over there to swim and blow money at the convenience store, and everyone would wind up happy.

In my rookie year, we were supposed to stay at the Campground, and we were excited about it at the time, but that was when it lit on fire.

Everything was on fire that year. The city of Timmins was almost evacuated, but not quite; some of the surrounding small towns were.

The first time I ever worked a burn block was the very end of that contract, right before we went parading off to Ottawa for the bender. The block was so freshly burned that there was nothing growing, and the bugs were almost — almost — not there, and little clouds of ash and smoke rose out of the ground when we opened it with our shovels. The ground was this homogenous dry black stuff — not quite soil nor ash nor organic matter, but everything all burnt up together — and the treeline was black standing lines like a barcode against the plain white sky, and everything smelled like a woodstove.

While working in that block I once paused to watch a helicopter pass overhead with a full bucket. I watched it nearly to the horizon, watched it release the contents of its gargantuan red bucket, and then fly back the way it came. My crew boss Amo came stomping out of nowhere, out of the smoke-scented barcode and into my land, and said,

What the fuck are you doing —

— Because I wasn't planting trees, and I wasn't even looking at the ground.

So I motioned for him to look and told him, Everything's on fire.

And he said, No, and he was a terrible liar. Amo looked at the helicopter dumping its bucket —

No, he said, It *was* on fire but they put it out now — Just plant trees, okay.

And many times the helicopter zoomed over my head, back and forth, and I stopped watching it, and I heard at the end of the day that we'd almost been called off work, because the fire had been so close to my crew. But it was the end of the contract and there was a push to finish, as there always is — a push to finish before the first of July — and they didn't call us off work, and nothing bad happened, anyway.

We finished the contract working in that burn block, and I remembered it with fondness — the ground all black, the air totally dead, and us coming out of it looking like chimney sweeps, smelling like campfire — and it was all very exciting, as things were.

29

But, again, these things do change.

The burn blocks changed. Two years after the fires, the black turned to green, and the green became our enemy.

Day 35: we awoke to the spectacle of Jurassic Park.

Twelve of us slept in the van; three were awake. Konrad was awake because he was driving, and Ben was awake, riding shotgun, because he was supposed to make sure Konrad was awake. Travis didn't need to be awake but he was anyway; he sat in the backseat and read books. Travis' fingers stained the pages black one at a time, so if you looked at the edge of the book you could see how far he'd read, based on the colour of the paper.

Day 35 twelve of us awoke at the entrance to the block, where the road was flooded and the bushes closed tight around it. The van went pitching like a boat at sea and the branches on either side cracked at the windows like whips. That was the wakeup call.

We had a moment of excitement when a hefty black bear appeared in front of us on the road and Konrad bore down on it; we all craned our necks to see out the windshield while the animal sprinted along — bulky and rippling and godaw-ful fast. Bears, same as moose, always run straight down the road for a while, try to outrun the vehicle, before veering off sideways.

This time, when the bear veered off the road, it dis-appeared immediately into the sea of green. The land all around us was high tangled bush — junk trees, for us, like poplar, and raspberry bushes, and some little spruce that had survived the fires — and all of it was tightpacked into a hard green wall that went on forever, chest-high, shoulder-high, or towering overhead. And as we drove — well, we weren't sure, yet — perhaps it would clear out somewhere — perhaps we weren't quite at the *block* yet — but I think we all knew, and we all kind of started to smile — darkly, this laughter fluttering in the space between rage and resignation. Laughter at the futility of it and laughter at the dread.

The suicide jokes started cracking. The guys started talking about how best to die before the day began —

Can someone smash my skull in with their shovel?

Only if you do it to me first.

We'd have to do it at the same time.

No, someone has to do it themselves — You have to stick your shovel in the ground with the blade up and jump on it — Get impaled.

Or I'll just chase that bear in there and try to get mauled.

Well, anyone who goes in there isn't coming out anyway — It's fucking full of bears — Bears and velociraptors — Fucking Jurassic Park.

By then everyone was awake, getting lively and getting mad, crazy-mad, and we heard Rodrigo up front, theatrical Rodrigo, loud and bantering with a rookie, telling him,

You're gonna have a fuck of a day in there, Dekkar — and fuck you completely, I wish you a FUCK of a day —

So the van was getting restless with this dark kind of energy — but hey, energy is energy and you plant trees on any kind of energy, so we went with it and it mounted.

Konrad tossed everyone out. Ben and Arron, first, because highballers always wanted to plant trees, and highballers wouldn't complain. Then the rest of us, two or three at a time, out on the roadsides with the caches. We knelt and shoved trees into our bags. Clipped in, maybe chugged some water, and went pounding through. Went slashing, cutting though, with everything ripping and whipping and smacking our faces —

And we couldn't see anything, in land like that: we were blind. Green overhead, green all around, green snagging us by the ankles and grabbing at our knees.

We'd just go smashing on through, and we'd drop flagger all over the place. Flagger was bright-coloured photodegradable tape that we dropped on our seedlings or tied up onto branches as we went, marking where we'd been and where we'd planted. In places like Jurassic Park, sometimes even the flagger was invisible after a while. Then we'd just put our heads down, eyes half-closed, try to move forward in a straight line. More or less.

30

I met the Client representative on the roadside that day. This guy, we all knew him; he'd had the same job for thirty years. He was the Client-Planter interface on their side. His priority was safety. He was really concerned with safety — I mean, really, quite.

The Client gave us a list of working directives, and it went like this: first Safety; then Quality; lastly, Production.

Our Company told us the same thing, over and over again: Safety, Quality, Production.

In our minds, as planters, it was the same list but backwards. Production: money, trees, money, more trees, more money, more bragging rights, more money, more trees.

Quality: prevent re-planting, because you won't be paid to re-plant bad trees — bad trees, less money.

Then Safety: a good joke — What is safety, when on one hand you're already broken and sick like a zombie, and at the same time you've already proven to be invincible?

Client was on the roadside chatting with Parks, leaning on the F250, when I came crashing out of the bushes midday. Eyes on the ground half-closed, swayed to the cache and knelt and drank water.

Hot sun, clear sky, greenness flashing and glinting like glass all around. The Client peered at me from a few metres away, glasses under his blue hard hat, and he told me,

Sorry about that.

Smiled, fatherly almost, like it was a good joke between the two of us. He was apologizing about the land.

No worries, I said.

I opened a bundle and started moving trees into my bag. Slowly, carefully, holding them with two hands, by the pods and not the stems — because the Client was watching.

He stood and watched me moving pods, and he said this:

At least we won't lose you in there.

He smiled.

I paused in my dawdling bag-up and looked at him, squinting against the sun, with my mind pretty blank under the heat of it, and I had no idea what he was talking about. We looked at each other for a second. Silence. I put my head back down, filled my bags and sorted out the plastic waste from the bundles, and then stood and strode past him and smashed into the wall of bushes.

Alone again in the murky green, while thrashing along, I made sense of what he said. At least we won't lose you in there, he said, because I was making so much noise flailing in the bushes. All of the planters were rustling the trees like little angry monsters invisible in the bush. So even if we lost ourselves in Jurassic Park, at least they wouldn't lose us.

Okay. Fine.

The Client rep was a really nice guy, a family man, religious. He certainly meant well. He was good at his job. If only he knew how much blind rage had been directed towards him, personally, over the course of those thirty years — raw fury, from all of those powerless planters enduring the worst days of their lives with no one else to blame for it — I wonder if he knew. Likely enough, he did.

I wasn't angry, not anymore. I'd been angry once in my rookie year, when the Client rep had stopped me mid-stride towards a Personal Best, by telling everyone that the trees were too deep in the sand. Then everyone had gone raging about it because — It's impossible not to plant trees deep in loose sand, we said, and FUCK THIS, we said, and FUCK HIM.

Anyway, that hadn't done much good, so eventually we'd had to stop shouting and just plant trees. And we'd learned to hold the seedlings by the stems while kicking them closed so that they wouldn't slide in too deep.

In Jurassic Park, Day 35, the Client rep apologized to me because it was supposed to be the Client's responsibility to prepare the land for us. Usually, with so much green growth, they would spray the land with chemicals to strip all the leaves off. Or rather, they would enlist *us* to spray it with chemicals. It was a planter's job for the off-season: spraycation. Dress up in gear and walk around with a tank on your back spraying chemicals on everything.

Chem-sprayed land wasn't green anymore. It was brown, bristly. It was thorn-coated stems all tangled together, as though the earth had grown a coat of matted, barbed fur.

The chem-spray was a way to protect the Client's investment; to help the seedlings survive by killing everything else.

I don't know, personally, what happened to all the seedlings we planted in Jurassic Park. I don't know how they'll fare against all the competition in that overgrown meadow. I'm no forestry professional.

I planted about six thousand trees in my piece of Jurassic Park. More or less they were two metres apart from each other in every direction, deep-tight-upright in mineral soil, because that was my job. The Client's quality checkers didn't go into the land, didn't try to find the trees, because it was too hard to walk in there.

31

After breaking my leg in the workshop, I was approached by a representative of the school's insurance company. The representative was a grey, gentle man, who had a kind of softness about him and spoke carefully. He asked me about the accident, about my leg, about my lifestyle.

He told me that, in technical terms, I was partially at fault for the accident, because I pulled the wood over. Technically, the school was also partially at fault, because the wood was stored incorrectly, adversely to the specified safety standards.

He told me that lawsuits happen all the time, that the school was insured and the school had lots of money, that my leg would never be the same and my quality of life would be affected by the accident, and the school was partially at fault for that. He advised me to sue the company he was representing.

I didn't sue. I joked about it, many times — like, If I'd sued the school I wouldn't have to be planting these fucking trees, you know — but when it came down to it, I never had any intention of starting a lawsuit.

The injury did have an effect on my quality of life. Yes. During my month's internment in Manitoba, a bunch of things went wrong. When that contract ended it was a soaring relief to me, because it felt like I couldn't have gone on any longer anyway.

The left calf was atrophied and tight and it pulled the ligament along my foot and gave me plantar fasciitis — a tearing sensation every time I took a step. I'd had a hole drilled into my knee, so the joint ached and complained. The screw in my ankle had gone through a nerve, and the scar tissue there was interfering with a tendon, making it difficult to use my left foot. I could feel this particular screw rubbing against the inside of my boot, and a patch on my ankle went numb.

The bone itself wasn't fully healed so there was a splintering pain emanating from the site of the break. On top of that, a bone spur had formed where the tibia had come out of the skin. Around the spur, the muscles seemed to be attached to the bone, and they tended to cramp up, searingly. And in the same spot, there was a nerve, somehow caught and isolated — so that if anything ever made contact with this bone spur, the resulting sensation was kind of like torture.

That was my list of complaints. I walked, and stomped, and carried loads on it; I planted through it for a month.

At the time, regarding that, I could only see two options —

One option was to blame the school for assuming that no one would be dumb enough to pull eight-hundred-pounds-worth-of-trees-and-glue over onto their own body. Then I would spend how-many-months in testing and testifying in order to prove myself crippled and victimized, unable to work, and complain about the injuries and the trauma for so many hours and so many days on end that, ultimately, it would lead to the phenomenon of becoming truly crippled and traumatized by force of sheer willpower.

That's very serious.

The other option was to go back to work. Move on. Get better. Get over it.

As it turned out, though, that was a difficult thing to do. It took me a long time.

By the time I got over it, fully, it was the 67th day of my third season of tree planting. It had been twenty-two months. That's how long, I think, it really took.

32

Following Jurassic Park, Yukon and Parks and Bennett started naming parts of the block after countries. It was a huge block, and it had all been on fire two years earlier, in the raging flames of my rookie season. Vast and sprawling, the block was a puzzle of interlocking sections and old narrow roads, and it kept us busy for a good long time.

The three deliverers were always the first ones there, and they were the ones who started making up names. They'd study the maps together, divide the terrain, decide on strategies and tactical moves. They'd meet to confer in the middle of the dirt roads, and they'd all assume the pose for talking business: one knee on the ground, and on the other knee one elbow propped up, and one hand holding a cigarette or an energy drink or both. That was the pose; those were the poisons.

It was during these conferences, or during their high-efficiency banter over the two-way radios, that all the sections of the burn block started to earn their names —

Switzerland was shaped like a cross on the map. Sudan was sandy as all hell. Japan was east of Korea.

There were two areas named after Korea, because the South section was so much more hospitable than the North.

I spent two days in Jurassic Park and then two days in North Korea, and to me they were the same thing. Four days of thrashing, of fighting, and cutting and whipping, red blood on the thorns and branches, and green bush all across my vision.

There were a few lovely moments when I saw the green sea differently — when I noticed, bending below the surface of thick growing leaves, that underneath the green there was a kind of suspended paradise, like underwater, where the sounds were different and the sunlight came in just barely, a tiny dappling on the soil — and I was completely alone and quiet and calm, and it was nice for half a second.

And then two more steps forward. Bent-backed and high-stepping through the jailcell web of branches — and again, and so on. It gets old.

So on the fifth day, on Day 39, I was excited to be in South Korea. The ground was low, the horizons clear. The brambles were knee-high brownish things, and from the treeline I could see all the way to the road. The blindfold was off.

Brilliant, lovely.

I was working next to a rookie highballer and both of us injured ourselves around the same time. Early morning, he stepped off a log and twisted an ankle. Both of us kept working all day anyway.

The grass and bushes were thick at ground level and required a lot of kicking — screefing, we called it — to expose the soil. It also required a heavy stomp to close each hole, since the grass and roots made the soil stiff, less pliable.

On my first bag-out of the day — my very first trip into the land — I had reached the treeline, planting at a happy pace, screefing and stomping with gusto, and then I turned around to head back to the road.

I planted ambidextrously, always, to save my wrists and shoulders from injury; of course I ended up with tendonitis in both elbows, but it would have been worse if it had just been one. So on my way back towards the road that morning, I swapped my shovel into my left hand, and I started stomping the holes closed with my left foot.

I kicked around and opened a hole in the ground with my shovel, left-handed, in a bunch of yellowy-white grass that was about knee-high. There was soil under the grass. I put a white spruce seedling there, and then tried to stomp the hole closed using quite a bit of force, and that's when I got hurt.

There was a log hiding in the yellowy-white grasses there: a piece of dry white rock-solid wood, with stumpy snapped-off branches radiating out of it. One of these branches was as thick as my wrist with a jagged tip like a spear, and this jagged tip was pointing up on a diagonal towards me.

I stomped down with the left leg. I threw all of my force into it. And as I did so, my shin happened to connect with the tip of this bone-hard stick — exactly on the site of the compound fracture.

For fuck's sake.

It was bad. It was actually really bad.

I doubled over and tried to swear but my breath caught in my throat and I just choked instead and stood there coughing, bent over, standing on one leg with the other one limp, and I held onto that godforsaken little stick and I tried to break it as an act of vengeance,

But my energy had gone out with my breath and I was just choking and coughing and holding this log-stump quite pathetically with my hands uselessly limp so I stopped trying to break it and hung there with my head reeling and heart pounding all over again because, what —

It was incredibly painful and made my whole body jolt into high-awareness mode and all I could do was bend over and cough, and feel it, all over again —

I hung there for a minute.

I stopped coughing, and my breathing relaxed.

A few more breaths.

And then what?

I put my left foot down, still leaning forward on the shovel. I rocked my weight onto my left leg. The shin smarted explosively.

It throbbed.

It held.

I kicked the hole closed with my right foot. Not very hard. The tree, I'm sure, was loose.

I rocked forward. Right foot forward. Rocked onto the left heel, rocked off of the left heel. Another tree.

Spine horizontal, right hand in the ground. Another tree. Another tree.

Another tree.

33

Injuries happened. Injuries were not uncommon, to say the least.

Shoulders, back, knees, wrists: they got overworked. Among the veterans, especially, there was a marked familiarity with the kind of clinging pain that would just grind on you, just pull and prod and melt you into a puddle of oozing indifference at the end of every day.

And we could always stop working, if we wanted to stop working—

Or we could continue working, if we wanted to get paid.

And even the planters who escaped the chronic problems—even the planters without sports injuries, tendonitis, pulled muscles, bad joints—

Well, everyone still knew about pain.

Stefan: he was as strong as a bull, apparently. That's what Yukon told me about him. They'd been friends since high school and they climbed mountains together, and Yukon told me that Stefan was unstoppable.

We were leaning on the tailgate of his F150, later in the season; I'd spent half the day at the hospital and was delivering with Yukon again instead of planting. The two of us worked until sunset that evening, but the planters were finishing up at the usual hour, and we stopped by Stefan's cache at the end of the day for a visit.

Stefan was walking out to the roadside, empty bags, and Yukon said to me,

I don't think he knows how strong he is, But he's like a bull, Nothing can stop him.

I watched him plodding along, eyes on the ground. Tall and long-limbed and fluid, in a way.

He doesn't really look it, I said.

And Yukon agreed — He doesn't look it, but he's unstoppable.

It was Stefan's third year of planting, same as me, and he'd never had one of those endless injuries — not yet. He planted prodigiously and almost effortlessly, or so it seemed to me, and he came out strong at the end of every day.

But despite any of that — despite any kind of fortitude, health, natural ability or grace — still everyone knew about pain.

A few days after my adventure in South Korea, the cool dim twilight found Stefan and I at the handwashing station after most of the planters had gone to bed — and I was lying flat on the gravel and watching the clouds overhead so that I didn't have to watch Stefan prying up a bloody fingernail with a pocketknife.

He was standing over the table where the cooks set out plastic basins of water and pump-dispensed soap. We were encouraged to wash our hands there once a day before dinner. The water would be opaque black after one or two people had done so.

Stefan had drawn himself a clean basin of water. He was using some soap and a broad-bladed knife to pick at the dirt that was clotted into the remains of his middle fingernail. The nail had been cracked by a rock while he was planting and it was split in half down the centre, with one side missing, blackened and raw. The remaining half of it was peeling upwards, leveraged off by a filling of hard-packed earth and blood.

He smiled when he showed it to me, smiled resignedly like a shrug.

Tomorrow's gonna suck, he said, and he laughed. His characteristic laugh, so deep it almost stayed in his throat.

How bad was it today? I asked.

Still smiling, another shrug:

You know how it is, You can't really feel it after a while.

Of course, that's exactly how it is. Always is.

I went to my tent to get a sewing needle, gave it to Stefan so he could use the needle instead of the knife. Then I lay down on the ground and faced the sky, and I let my limbs go limp against the flat-packed gravel, and we talked for a while.

That was the day Stefan had given me a little Ziploc bag with three caffeine pills in it, as a trial run. He'd told me that the caffeine had made a huge difference for him, while planting. One pill in the morning, he said, Sometimes one more in the afternoon — and it meant something like a hundred more dollars a day, for him. It was an easy wakeup call, something to get his head in the game right away.

As I lay flat on the ground that evening, watching the clouds go dark, I smiled about it and told Stefan:

I'm not going to take caffeine; I don't want to rely on it.

And I told him: I was in my land today, and I was really happy for no reason whatsoever — I was just happy to be planting trees — So, fuck the caffeine, I don't need it.

Stefan glanced up from his finger and he smiled, low and half-satirical —

That must be nice, he said, Must be really fucking nice.

He looked back down, picked carefully with the needle, still smiling — and I smiled up against the sky.

§ § § §

And, sure, it was nice, for a while. I liked being drug-free, as a planter. I felt, somehow, like I was doing it right: I didn't need any artificial motivation.

In terms of artificial motivation, caffeine was the lightest thing out there. In terms of taking whatever you could — in terms of putting everything on hold for the sake of the paycheck —

There were planters taking caffeine — one pill, two pills, five pills a day — and there were planters taking non-prescription painkillers. There were also planters who were stoned all the time. And there were also planters who were taking Adderall, Ritalin, Vicodin, Tylenol-with-codeine: for focus and for numbness — for a better paycheck — for a way to make the days slide smoothly by.

All of it was temporary, you know. The planting season was temporary. It wasn't real. For the most part, the planters who were taking pills would stop cold-turkey as soon as the season was over. It was only for the money. It was only in the bush, and the bush wasn't real.

It was the same with cigarettes: a lot of the smokers would quit entirely at the end of every season. And alcohol, too— maybe the drinking would level out, once the summer was over. Or maybe not.

In my third season of planting, I didn't want to rely on any drugs. I didn't want to find myself craving any kind of buzz. I was practicing, I was keeping my own head in the game, and I thought I was doing a pretty good job of that.

But as it goes, I spoke too soon. There comes a certain point, you know, when such vague abstract principles start to take a back seat. There comes a certain point when you find that you actually do not give a fuck — not a fuck whatsoever.

And after that point you just take what you can get.

34

After I smashed my leg in South Korea I continued to plant trees. I rocked on and off my left side, carefully, and I listened to the shouting of my nervous system and I wondered if I'd injured the bone again. When a bramble brushed the front of my shin, the impact almost brought me to my knees. A swipe from a blade of grass struck me like a lightning bolt.

My planting bags were half-full of trees. I planted my way back to the roadside. Carefully. One step at a time.

At the road I unclipped and started bagging up slowly, leaned over one-legged without kneeling. I ploddingly moved trees into my bags and thought quietly about my shin.

I thought about my options. The options were to stop planting or to continue planting.

Konrad roared up in the van and leapt out, all excitement and energy. He asked how my day was, asked if I was having fun, and I said, Yeah, I'm feeling fucking great —

Which was true, actually, because the mania was already coming on, because I'd already made my decision, then — and I knew I was going to plant trees all day. I was tired of favouring my leg and I was beginning to find the whole thing ridiculous, so I let the mania flood in and I told Konrad, I'm feeling fucking great right now.

He said, Good, and he made as if to leave and I said —

Wait — I need a shinpad.

A shinpad?

Yeah, I told him, I think I broke my leg.

Your broken leg?

Yeah, that one.

You broke it?

Maybe, maybe not, maybe — I need a shinpad.

Konrad was smiling — as always. He liked the prospect of problem-solving; he was an engineer, after all.

We tossed some ideas around as I bagged up, and then Konrad went into the van and came out with a bus-driving manual. It was a little paperback book, landscape-format, content approved by the Ministry of Transportation of Ontario. I held it curved in a semicircle over my shin, and Konrad duct-taped it against my legging. One strip of tape wrapped twice around the top, and another strip around the bottom, right above my boot, with the bright-purple book-back and the white italic government jargon showing through in between.

And we grinned at each other and I said, Yeah This is Fucking Great.

He gave me a pat on the back and his blue-eyed Konrad smile, and he went trundling off in the van, and I went trundling back into the land.

It was a great day.

It took me a long time to realize — I mean, weeks afterwards — to realize that I'd spent that whole afternoon bombing around on a massive adrenaline rush, and that's why it was so great.

It was insane, it was lovely.

At first I thought the shinpad wouldn't work. There was a swelling growing already, this hard swollen lump coming up out of the fracture site. When I taped the shinpad on, the plasticky backing of the book pressed against the swelling, and I thought maybe that hurt too much.

But after a few steps — as Stefan said — You know how it is, You can't really feel it after a while.

And then my leg was protected from the grass and brambles and sticks, and I started to be invincible.

The afternoon was fully euphoric. All I did was plant trees — as always — and I didn't take any drugs at all, but I went smashing around heedlessly, and I felt like there was nothing I'd rather be doing. One tree after another after another — my whole body electric with shock — the sensation of wet earth on my hands and the fresh lungfuls of cloudy air — and motion, running rolling motion, like a dance to the music that was pounding in my ear —

Wow, it was great.

35

We were all planting spruce that day. We were all planting spruce for a while.

Jurassic Park, North Korea, South Korea: it was wettish greenish land. Jack pine wouldn't grow there, so the Client had prescribed the land for spruce.

On Day 34 we planted the last of the sun-thawed jack pine seedlings, and for the next eight days we planted black and white spruce only.

The spruce wasn't moldy; it was all springy green and alive.

By coincidence, on Day 41, I found that I was no longer coughing up phlegm. My sinus infection cleared up, too.

Perhaps I can't speak for anyone else — perhaps I can't be sure — but I imagined that the staccato hack-hacking across the gravel was quieting down, easing up.

And I found that I could breathe again.

36

On the day that I smashed my shin the contract was about halfway done. At the end of that day, I was wondering if I'd rebroken the bone and if so what I should be doing about that.

I wondered about it on the ride home that evening, and during dinner, and then I sought out some advice.

The closest thing I could find to a medical professional was B. He'd planted for five years and was now a crew boss, and in the real world he was a licensed paramedic. He worked as an emergency responder on ski hills in the winter. I wanted to ask B about my leg but he was out front of the Management Trailer having some kind of a lively conversation with Tom. The two of them — shoulder-length hair and bandanas and dirty once-white t-shirts — a gritty pair of bona fide bush veterans, sending laughter noises out across the gravel.

I waited, because I didn't want to approach Tom, because I thought he was kind of intimidating. He was too far above me in the ranks.

I told Skobie this — told her, I want to talk to B but he's talking to Tom.

Skobie was in the circle of plastic chairs out front of the mess tent for the Rookie Meeting. I sat on the ground in front of her, leaned against her legs and let my mind wander off while Arron and Andreas gave a mentoring session about the proper use of flagger in overgrown land. Periodically I turned around to glance at where Tom and B were, fifty metres away leaning on the silver F350, and I waited for them to separate. They kept laughing.

It was getting late and I wanted to go to bed. The ground was hard and my whole body was sore and it was cold and windy out. I waited until the rookie meeting was letting up. I complained to Skobie. As the rookies were standing and stretching and yawning or smoking and moving about, Skobie told me not to be a pussy about it and then she started yelling across the gravel pit towards B, who was her crew boss.

Tom and B stared at us. What?

So I had to walk over to them and explain.

I addressed B:

If I broke a bone before, is it more likely to re-break now? Or less likely?

I don't know, he said, I've never broken a bone before.

Oh.

Why? He asked.

Yeah, just, I broke my leg once and I smashed it today pretty hard, and I don't know if I might have fractured it again, or something.

B looked at me blankly, and said, You just walked all the way over here without limping at all.

Tom smiled. He was looking elsewhere.

And I said something like, Yeah —

— Because it was true; I hadn't been limping, but then I'd had twenty months of practice not-limping; I'd never limped, because it wasn't my knee that hurt, it was just my shin for fuck's sake and you can always use your shin without limping, if you want to. And I didn't know what else to say — just, Yeah.

Did you plant on it all day?

Yeah, I taped a book over it.

What book?

A bus manual.

Why did you have a bus manual?

It was Konrad's bus manual.

Tom and B were smiling — they glanced at each other. I somewhat rolled my eyes and said,

I don't know — I just wanted to see if you knew if it might be broken because you're a paramedic apparently.

He asked to see it and I showed him. Hardly discoloured, it was just a swollen lump, a hard mound gently rising, on the left edge of the fracture scar and the tender bone spur. There wasn't much to see.

B shrugged.

I don't know, he said — If you can plant on it, just keep planting on it, and if it gets worse go see a doctor.

Yeah, I said, I guess so.

Then Tom spoke: And make sure you tape a book over it every day, And make sure you tape a book over it at night, too — That'll help for sure.

I looked at him. Um.

And make sure you use a different book at night, he said slowly half-smiling, Because you never want to sleep in your work clothes —

I turned around and walked away, not-limping, while the guys started laughing behind me, and I went to my tent and went to sleep. And in the morning I woke up and planted trees, and I did the same thing the day after that, and the same thing for more than a month after that.

37

At the end of every contract there was always a push to finish — Finish hard Finish fast Finish on time — All the trees need to get gone, quick.

Often the supervisor would give us reasons for this — he or she would find something motivating to say, to help up the urgency factor. Part of the explanation, of couse, was just the ethos of the job: high-efficiency high-production high-earnings high-speed — and glory, you know, right at the end. Then there were other reasons, or explanations, that would appear with the circumstances.

In my rookie contract, Northern Ontario, we needed to finish before Canada Day so that the Company didn't have to give us holiday pay. My second contract, New Brunswick, needed to end before the Civic Holiday for the same reason.

My third contract, Manitoba, needed to end because we were being evicted from the campsite. I don't know if we ever had permission to be there. It was a clearing in the bush on the shoulder of a railway line.

On my first night in that campsite, three in the morning, there was this raging roaring noise like a thousand helicopters breaking up the sky and foggy lights blaring through the wall of my tent, kaleidoscoping shadows out of tree branches, and then a blasting screaming siren-noise. The first time it happened I thought it was an alien invasion or a helicopter squad.

It wasn't.

At three in the morning or so, the train liked to slow to a halt beside us and blast its horn. So the second time it happened, and the third, and the rest of them, it was just another thing to ignore. Just another thing to mumble about conversationally in the mornings, while huddled in layers against the clouds of mosquitoes above the breakfast tables.

Then we got evicted and had to finish the contract before the end of July. So we did.

The final day of that season, I thought that maybe it was my last day of tree planting forever, and that felt bittersweet.

Evidently I was wrong about that.

As I was planting that day, things started to feel really weird. I felt the ground tilting towards me, double-speed, when I bent over, and everything seemed too close and too high-contrast. I kept expecting someone to come up behind me and I wasn't sure why but I kept looking back over my shoulder. The shadows around me were getting too heavy and there was this darkness in my head that somehow matched the black of the treeline and it felt like the black was going to creep out of my skull and over my eyes and cover everything. I stood up and felt my brain roll backwards like a ball-bearing and I heard someone calling my name, a tinny washed-out voice, and I knew there was no one out there calling my name. The clouds were getting heavy and the air was stifling with oncoming storm and I was wondering how I'd gotten stoned because I hadn't smoked anything, hadn't drank anything, and wasn't even working hard enough to be heatfucked.

Took out my bugspray then and sprayed it around my face, in a circle avoiding the eyes and lips. The bugspray was a different type than normal. The little hole-in-the-wall hardware store in Flin Flon had been sold out of the usual 30% poison and I'd had to spring the extra dollar for this fancy stuff. It smelled like cheap perfume and was supposed to be non-greasy.

And as I was spraying it, I caught a whiff of that unfamiliar chemical cocktail, and I decided that's probably what was messing with my brain.

So I sprayed it all over my neck and arms and then kept planting. When I'd finished that load of trees, I staggered back out to the road and stood there feeling slightly lopsided — then realized that one of my bags was still full and I'd only planted half. Then I had to go back in, feeling confused and a little bit scared and extremely discouraged.

Towards the end of that long heavy day the clouds opened and the mosquitoes got replaced with raindrops in the air. The thunder started to roll as we were all finishing up in the last piece of land, planting out the last few trees with high high speed because it was finally finally over, and we wanted to get the hell out of there. Cosmic cymbal-crashes had just begun to echo and flash in the sky when we loaded the vans, sopping wet and muddy, and went home for the party.

I think it was the most spectacular party I'd ever witnessed.

The thunder and the lightning kept rolling, as hard as a storm can be, and our boys were shooting off fireworks from the cliffsides all around so that everything was lit in flashes —

Orange light caught in the raindrops, streaking the sky with reflections of the fire. The fire was made out of the par-rafin-coated cardboard tree boxes — it was an inferno the size of a bungalow — and overhead the red and blue sparks were shooting out, the explosions competing with the thunder, and often enough the whole scene was lit up with a flash of hard lightning — and the sky above was completely, completely black with the clouds — starless, moonless fiery night —

We were raging inside of a massive hollowed-out pit at the bottom of this abandoned quarry. The vans were parked beside the fire and they were blasting, blasting music that was competing and meshing into some furious pounding white noise — white noise bouncing off the sheer cliffsides that rose around us on all sides — these shining-slippery rock walls that the crazy ones were climbing all over, stopping on ledges to dangle their legs off and shoot fireworks out over us —

Someone had a boat, a wooden canoe, and they brought it into the middle of the black-mirror lake beyond the fire, and they built a mast and a sail on it with the parrafin-cardboard tree boxes. Someone waded out and doused it all in gasoline, then came back to the shore — and we all watched while he shot a Roman Candle at it and everything blew up — flames dancing high against the cliffsides and flames spilling out across the black-orange water, psychedelically rippling, and everyone hollering like maniacs.

There was a chant that someone started — Burn Your Shirt — Burn Your Shirt — so that one at a time everyone was being singled out and pointed at and chanted at until they sent their shirt into the fire — shirt, pants, jacket, bra — anything and everything — so everyone was half-naked in the rain, skin getting scorched where it faced the inferno, and drenched through everywhere else.

Everyone was really, really drunk and pretty damn excited and it went on and it went on.

The following day we woke up drunk in tents and tore down camp — the least efficient Camp Move I've ever witnessed — with people dropping off and rambling away as fast as they could. We spent one final night in the motel at The Pas. We weren't really allowed to party there because they kicked us out of the hotel rooms when we got loud, they closed the bars when we came around, and they sent in the police, and then our guys would wake up in the drunk tank.

So in the end, it was supposed to be just one more quiet night in The Pas, but instead everyone got drunk again and stayed awake all night. Really, no one slept at all, because everyone was so in love with each other that they didn't want to waste the hours that were left —

Not me, though. I didn't care. I'd only known the guys for two weeks; these were the ones who'd just shown up to bail us out — the Rolligon crew — and I didn't care about any of them and I told them all that. I said, Eh, Fuck off, I want to go to sleep —

Maybe the novelty was already wearing off by then. It had been a hard month.

But still I couldn't go to sleep all night because there were so many people sitting on my bed and playing guitar and drinking Red Bull and crying.

This went on for a while. The Company convoy went to Edmonton to leave the vans in the yard there, so we went with them for the free ride, because the work was done and over, and there was nowhere else to be.

It took us two days to get to Edmonton, driving across Saskatchewan. It was a beautiful blessed ride: finally we were able to relax, finally finally able to just be still. I was sideways on top of the bags and tents and bedding piled up in the backseat. Sharing the seat with me was this guy Nigel, who'd been crying that morning while saying goodbye to the rest of his crew. Half-drunk and sleep-deprived, with red-rimmed eyes and tears soaking into his bushy ginger beard — Nigel was wearing a kimono emblazoned with a dragon, over top of a short denim dress—and I'm sorry, but I laughed aloud at the sight of him. He was crying because he didn't want to part ways with anyone, and he was wearing a dress and a kimono because it was comfortable, I suppose. He wore that getup all the way across Saskatchewan, and in the backseat of the van I had to keep telling Nigel to pull his fucking dress down because there was way too much of his white thighs blinding me.

The license plates in Saskatchewan called it The Land of Living Skies. I watched upside down out the back window: streaky pink sunrise fading into clear open blue, flat white clouds over the prairies and then the sun going down huge and heavy and red while the sky erupted with colours—and I slept in the back of the van that night, alone in the cold windy darkness, in the parking lot of a motel that I didn't want to pay for—and another sunrise and another sunset, living skies and blissful repose, and nothing but a bit too much of Nigel's thighs.

The license plates in Manitoba called it Friendly Manitoba. I think they couldn't think of anything better to say about the buzzing swamplands and the longest-running Murder Capital of Canada.

So onto Alberta—Wild Rose Country. Our destination after the ecstasy-fueled nights in Edmonton was an acid bender in Jasper National Park. The acid connection fell through, but twelve of us went anyway. We rented a van and pitched a camp under the tall pine trees by a greenish glacier-fed river and the mountains beyond. We woke up in the mornings to the sound of the water bubbling and the sound of beer cans cracking, cracking up the quietude of the rockies. We had beer for breakfast, whiskey for lunch, and on it went. The girls were still looking for acid, and someone found these posters in town that said: Lost Unicorn, If Found Please Call, with a phone number listed. Sara called the number at 2 am because, she said, Certainly there are drugs; she called and asked the guy for acid. No? Mushrooms? Ecstasy? Anything? Nothing, and please take the poster down — shitty prank.

I left the planters in Jasper and I went west alone, and it all carried on.

My ride to Vancouver was in a 1976 hand-painted motor-home named Big Mama. The driver was a forty-year-old funeral director who'd just resigned in order to roam the highways in an RV. The other passenger was his cousin, a single mother of one who'd left the kid somewhere else to take a break and an acid bender.

So I stumbled into the acid bender by accident and spent two days in an RV park in Kelowna with these two complete strangers, surviving on rum&coke and watching the sand by the lake ripple in giddy swirling patterns just like the clear green water, and on it went.

I met Arron near Vancouver. He wasn't planting trees that season. That was the season when Konrad was promoted to crew boss and Arron meanwhile worked in an actual architecture firm and started a career. But tree planting paid better, much better, so he came back for another season after that to kill off his student debt.

Arron and I pitched my tent in the backyard of someone's friend-of-a-friend on an island off the coast and a party sprung up around us. Everywhere I went that month, I swear, these mad flailing people kept gathering like storm clouds — I was a fast-moving party magnet.

In Lake Louise I stayed with a friend at a resort; I slept on a loveseat in a sticky dormitory where the windows were screwed shut to keep the staff from committing suicide. I got kicked out of the bar on my first night there, apparently, and the party wound up out under the stars just like always. It carried on, and we drank all day, cliff-diving into a pine-bordered lake somewhere off the highway, and we hitchhiked over to Banff just to get drunk on top of a mountain, and back again in the sunset, picked up by a professor of engineering from Waterloo, backseat full of camping gear—

I flew to Toronto from Calgary. I caught a flight, hungover at midnight on my birthday; I turned twenty-one somewhere in the vast dark skies above Friendly Manitoba, and when I landed I took three city buses and trains, three hours north into the suburbs—into the stagnant rows-and-rows-and-rows north of Toronto. I made a call from a payphone at a bus stop and was rescued there by a three-car party convoy, going north to cottage country. Pitched my tent again in the backyard at a friend's family cottage, and the party sprung up like a pop-up book—different people, different province, same thing that just kept going on, and how long had it been—how long had it been since I went to sleep for a few hours—

August went out on its own, still burning hot and heavy, dying explosively like a sunset over Saskatoon—and abruptly, accidentally, September began.

Ottawa, again: well-dressed people shaking soft hands with each other—big words, lofty phrases—talkative, straightbacked adults all calm and certain and delicately focused.

Eight more months of academia and at the end of it I was broke or a bit beyond broke, and I told Konrad that I needed a job.

One more year, I said—just one more season and then I'm out.

38

At the Campground, this season, things began to blur together again. Forty-five days we were there: forty-five-or-so
mornings, with routines becoming rituals.

Stefan and I were in the mess tent early, up before six.
Stefan wore a thrift-store bathrobe, held a mug of coffee in
one hand, and he wandered sedately about the mess tent as
though it was his own living room. Every morning when we
passed we said Good Morning to each other — every day just
before 6 am.

On one morning, Stefan said this:

I say more Good Mornings here than I ever do anywhere
else — But this is the only place where I actually mean it.

Each morning we each stuffed a bag full of lunch food.
Vanessa and Ceilidh laid out the lunch at the back of the mess
tent, across the aisle from the heated breakfast trays. They
laid out everything — everything in copious quantities and a
pretty heavy variety — sandwich ingredients, sugary treats,
sliced fruit, bagged leftovers. Each morning the tables would
be swarmed by planters, and each morning we practiced it
like a dance routine. We dodged and turned around each
other, dipping and weaving between arms and shoulders to
snatch up whatever we could. Watermelon was the hottest of
commodities; cantaloupe was the consolation prize for late
risers.

At the beginning of the season I'd sit down to share a lei-
surely breakfast with the early crew like Stefan, Buldyke,
Rodrigo — and we'd sit and talk and have some time to kill.
Later on I couldn't do it anymore; I couldn't be bothered to
sit down because I couldn't be bothered to stand up after;
and I couldn't be bothered to eat off a dish because I couldn't
be bothered to wash it after. Instead I'd grab an apple or a

handful of bacon and scarf it down while pacing in the aisle. That was all I could be bothered to do.

A lot of the mornings, the talk was on dreams. At breakfast, you know, nothing much had changed since the last time we'd all talked. All we'd done since dinner was sleep and dream, so often enough the dreams were the only news to tell.

Dreams were planting dreams. We planted trees all day and we planted trees all night. All of us, all the time. Even in the off-season; planting dreams were madly tenacious. Planting dreams — dreams about furrows that simply don't end. Dreams about wandering the woods while saddled with a bottomless set of planting bags. Dreams about planting things that aren't trees, about planting strange objects into paved streets. Dreams that wake you feverishly in the night because you need to plant the floor of your tent. Dreams about pockets of soil inside your sleeping bag, dreams about bundles of trees under the hood of your car. Dreams about stuffing trees into a grilled-cheese sandwich and eating it just to make them disappear.

That last one was Megan's. Personally, I've never had that particular dream. But I had a good laugh over it, anyway.

Megan and I met every morning at a quarter to seven. We were always the first ones ready. Fifteen minutes before the meeting, we'd be sitting in a pair of chairs outside the mess tent and we'd be laughing.

Megan and I barely needed to speak to each other. Mostly we communicated telepathically, or sometimes with a grin and a raised eyebrow. In general, Megan wasn't known for speaking much anyway; she was a wallflower with a reputation for being quiet. And simultaneously, quietly, she was the camp's female highballer at the end of that season.

In the mornings we sat outside and spat toothpaste into the gravel and we wrapped our boots in duct tape, and we sat, waited, sipped water. We'd exchange a word or two, here and there, and we would laugh, and we would laugh. Laughter was more critical than dialogue.

At 7 am the morning meeting would start, and the meeting circle would form around our chairs. People would carry more chairs out from around the breakfast tables, or they'd sit on the ground to lace their boots, or they'd stand behind and lean on the chairs in front. Clad in jackets and hoods and boots, coffee or water or cigarette in hand.

Tom would talk. He'd stand in front of the rising sun, every time, and no one could actually look at him without being blinded. We'd sit with our eyes on the ground or on each other, and he'd tell us about the trees, the nursery, the client, the weather, the block, the land, the quality, the schedule. Often enough he'd go rambling off into other territory — still in the same slow drawl, half-smiling at most. He'd start telling stories and he'd get everyone noisy and clapping and cheering over it. He'd make it a public announcement if an unlikely couple shacked up on a Night Off. He drew out a whole scenario and asked us, like:

Should we fire the rookie for sleeping with her crew boss — Or should we fire the crew boss for puking in her bed afterwards?

In answer to that, there was rowdy laughing-stomping-shouting. No one was fired.

Mail somehow became a theatrical event. There were letters and care packages from home: Tom went into town and picked them up, and he handed them out during the meetings. He'd call out the names — the lucky winners — and shake their hands ceremonially while the rest of us applauded and cheered.

Profoundly nonchalant, he half-satirically half-smiled:

Congratulations to all recipients ... And for the rest of you, Better luck next Mail Drop.

We had our rituals together, those forty-five days. We had a whole culture blooming.

Around Day 41, there was another event to add to our routine. Megan and I squeezed it into our schedule, as a bit of entertainment during the sessions of boot-lacing and tooth-brushing: the new event, each morning, was watching Korry squeeze pus out of the infection on her shin.

It was the same thing that she'd squeezed out of Mandog's forearm, a month prior. Buldyke had one too, and Rodrigo was growing one on his wrist. Andreas had one on his thigh, Bennett on his knee. And there were a few more, floating around the camp. We didn't have a solid diagnosis on these things but we'd realized, at least, that they were contagious.

Korry's infection was red and angry. It swelled out of the front of her right shin, a pink-purple mountain that was wider around than a golf ball. In the centre it was deep hard black, like a smashed thumbnail. She'd squeeze it, hard, and I could see pain when I looked at her leg, and I could see pain when I looked at her face, so sometimes I looked away.

But sometimes I would watch, and I would see the thick goo come crawling out of her stretched-shiny skin. She'd squeeze with her blackstained cracked-knuckle hands and wipe the pus away with a tissue. She'd put a glob of antibacterial cream under antiseptic gauze. She'd wrap a few layers of duct tape around her bare leg to keep the gauze in place — so every morning there would be a band of whitishness around her dirt-smeared leg, a band of almost-cleanness where the duct tape had been the day before.

We'd watch her tape it up and pull her pant leg back down. Then the three of us — Korry and Megan and I — would sit and wait for the morning meeting, and we'd grin and we'd laugh again, and the routine would go carrying on.

39

Following Korea we spent four days in Japan. It was another section of burn block, just east of where we'd been.

Black shining logs strewn across the ground, red and green mosses shooting out in between. The massive twisted stumps there had their soot-faced roots exposed where the soil had eroded away, after the forests were cut down. There were graveyards of round white stones and soft patches of ash on the ground. There were tangled tan branches of raspberry and, where the chem-spray had been missed or rained away, there were thickets of glinting poplar.

The roads to Japan were deep and sandy, and the van got stuck a lot. We'd tumble out, then, blinking half-alive into the white daylight, and we'd get behind, at the back or the open side doors, and we'd push, push, while the wheels spun and spewed sand around. Roll forward six inches. Put sticks and logs under the wheels for traction. Push and spin and push — Let's try backwards — push and roll backwards six inches — move the sticks and push again.

After this went on for a while, it seemed as though Konrad found a new technique to navigating the road. It seemed as though he simply stopped using the brakes. We'd fly around the bends, against the ditches and branches tight on either side, and in the backseat we'd be hitting our heads on the roof. The road rattled the van, clattered so loudly that it was hard to talk over, and I could feel the rattling inside of my left leg. It was like the noise jumped right inside of my bone, and I could feel it buzzing in there, somewhere between ticklish and painful.

Konrad asked me how my leg was doing. I told him maybe it was broken. He'd usually ask once a day.

Ten hours passing by, with one or two little dialogues to break the silence. Once a day, Konrad and I would have the same conversation, and then it would linger in the air even after that and chase me around — more and more meaningless each time until he stopped asking —

How's the leg? It's totally fucked.

How's the leg? It's fucked.

How's the leg? It hurts.

How's the leg? It functions.

How's the leg? It's a leg.

Plant a tree, plant another tree. There was nothing else to be done or said about that. There was no reason to say anything unless it was important, logistical — trees, land, vehicles — and otherwise it was a joke, it was something obscene.

How's the leg? It's fucking great.

It's fucking great, it's fucking great —

Mornings, evenings, trees, steps, words, music.

Music, all on repeat. I fell into time with one single album, twelve songs that I listened to on repeat. Every day I could hardly wait to put this beat into my ear and hammer along within the hammering of the music. Always in my right ear and not the left, always the same. All day without fail, the same twelve songs. By the end of the contract, I'd listened to the same twelve songs about three hundred times in a row. Three hundred times on repeat, and nothing else, ever.

My leg is fucking great, I said. Fucking great, I bent down and bent down.

Bent down a thousand more times and the album would start over.

Fucking great —

And I started to go faster. There was a lot of pain and perhaps it was adrenaline — again — that made me go faster. I kept falling over.

I stepped on uneven ground, I twisted the ankle slightly — and my left leg would fold and I would be on my knees. Inconvenient. Climbed up, heavily, staggered upright just to bend over again.

Bend over, bend over and the album started over.

I walked out of my land and folded onto the roadside by accident. Glanced up and saw Konrad down the road, on the quad, and he was looking at me.

I stood, again, upright and walked back to my cache, and at my cache I folded again, but deliberately this time. Konrad roared up and accused me — smiling, smiling again —

I saw you sit down on the road there —

And I told him,

I didn't sit down, I fucking bailed and ate shit.

And he didn't say anything. Smiling again, shrugging again, he roared off again.

I started to go faster.

While drunk on our Night Off in camp, that shift, I told Konrad that I would hit a Personal Best the following day. That would be our final day in Japan.

And so I did. I'd started to go faster.

Rolling hills in red and green, thorny sticks and twisted bare-black roots.

I stabbed the ground, stabbed the ground. I found soil in little pockets between the round-white stones. Little pockets of soil to bury the roots of the next generation, the roots of the white spruce and white spruce and white spruce and white spruce, between the roots of the twisted black stumps where the soil was eroding away.

The same twelve songs on repeat, and I started to fly.

White spruce, another white spruce, and the album started over.

I walked out of my land around 4 pm, out onto the sandy-rocky path winding between the burns of Japan. The road was endless and grey and empty. The sky was bare and blue and also endless, also empty. One of my legs was buzzing in a strangely half-numb manner — endlessly buzzing, oddly empty of sensation. I straightened my back and walked, and the album started over.

Shouldered my gear and walked out. One step then another. One leg was buzzing. One ear was full of the same predictable sounds, and the other was empty like the sky and the road.

There was no one on the road. A kilometre or two before I ran into a few other planters, and they'd run of land, too. Konrad was nowhere to be found. We walked, together. We cattle-planted: we planted together, side-by-side.

Bend over, bend over, shovel in the ground. Seven planters in a row, seven shovels in the ground. Fourteen steps at a time, and again. Sun rolled across the empty sky. Seven shovels in the ground. The album started over.

We could see the van, once we'd made it far enough — once we'd made it close enough to the entrance of Japan. The van was perched up high, shiny flashing white and stationary, and it was stuck deep, deep in the sand — again. It was a tiny white glint on the horizon, across all those rolling red-green hills still unplanted, still charred and treeless with the soil slowly trickling away. Seven of us trickling slowly along. The sun slowly trickling down.

A deliverer arrived to tow the van out of the sand, and the bumper ripped right off the front of the van.

Seven of us in a row, bending over, and the album started over.

One leg was buzzing — one hour and then another — a thousand white spruce, another thousand white spruce.

I hit my Personal Best, that day. Sure. The seven of us didn't finish working until Japan was full of white spruce. The seven of us and Konrad, we made it home after 9 pm, with the front bumper lying on the floor of the van and the license plate perched on the dashboard. We rolled home to an emptying mess tent. Both ears finally empty of music, and full sporadically of dialogue. One leg, now, less numb. Feelings started to return: exhaustion and hunger and smiles and words. I went to sleep that night and when I woke up the leg was much less numb. Much less numb, and instead explosive.

So I broke the routine that day, after Japan. I didn't roll home in the van with the license plate in the windshield on Day 45. I went to the hospital instead.

40

Three of us went to the hospital that evening, and all for different reasons. Korry and Maddie went with Konrad after dinner, and I went with Yukon straight from the block.

Korry went because she needed a prescription for antibiotics. The infection on her shin was massive, red-black and throbbing, and it wasn't getting any smaller. She picked up a bottle of pills that she was supposed to take multiple times daily.

Maddie went alongside Korry, because she'd been knocked out completely by heat exhaustion. Maddie was one of the toughest girls I've known, and she was too sick that evening to eat or drink. She'd spent a good chunk of the afternoon sitting in the passenger seat of Yukon's truck, asleep. To try and stay lucid, she'd picked up the book on the dashboard and started reading. The book was *Canada's Weather*, which Yukon had bought at the mall in Timmins because that's the kind of thing he read for fun. Maddie had tried (and failed) to stay awake through the heat exhaustion, by reading out paragraphs detailing the formation of freezing rain.

The freezing rain was on its way by then. The storm hit two days later, on the last day of June. Until then the sun was mean and the air was suffocatingly hot and ever-heavier.

41

It struck on the day before Canada Day. The timing was convenient enough for my crew, since we were heading into town midday for the holiday, just as the storm was breaking over us — but it was far less convenient for the crews that got stuck in it.

Canada Day: that was the one when I finally talked to Ben, after a full two years of nothing much. We were at the club and, sure, I was pretty drunk when I asked him —

Hey, what happened?

We hadn't really spoken all season. Ben sat quiet in the front seat of the van every day. He planted a whole lot of trees, he popped caffeine and snapped at rookies, and he never seemed to smile and I told him I missed his smile. He was crusty, as we say — A Crusty Vet — a veteran that's so hard they're barely there.

He grew up. He told me: I grew up.

So did I, said I — and then he laughed at that, and so did I, because I guess only one of us had changed.

He told me he was there for money — I'm only here to plant trees — He told me that if he wanted to be having fun he could plant a thousand fewer trees every day and maybe he'd be having more fun, but what's the fucking point of that —

And I wasn't really sure, but something felt wrong about that —

— to me, something felt wrong —

But what do you say? No one has time for romantics.

The romance fades: a veteran told me that, once. She'd spent five years in the bush, and then she told me that she wasn't coming back. Five years was enough. The romance fades, she said — and I was a rookie then, in love with the east-coast summer, and I thought it was kind of sad.

But it's true. It's true if you've been there long enough. Once the freedom loses its novelty, once you aren't so excitable anymore —

Once you've been there long enough, then you might find that you're a budding alcoholic and you're slowly breaking down. Your back will never be the same and you have nothing else to fall back on. You have no employable skills, you don't know any real people, and your university degree won't get you a job.

Most importantly, there's no way to make the same kind of money doing anything else.

So you whore yourself out, one more season, just to scrape by for one more year.

And then maybe another.

And, sure, it might cease to be exciting. I know, I know that. Eventually you might not feel excited, because the only thing you can feel is that you are very fucking tired. And instead of being in love — in love with the freedom or the novelty or the people in the job — you might find that you are simply in pain.

It can become a jail sentence, in many ways — a self-imposed jail sentence, and maybe that's the worst part. You did it to yourself. For months at a time, you drop your own reality and walk away — walk away from your relationships, your home and your hobbies; your progress, your thoughts and your goals. You walk away from any interest you might have had in your own health and wellbeing, so that you can spend every day doing something you hate, and every night sleeping or drinking it off.

The only thing to justify that is the money. You have to be there for the money: you have to make it lucrative, at least — at the very least.

Ben told me: I'm not here to have fun — (not anymore) —

And what do you say to that? It was true.

He won, in the end. He won the whole race, highballed the camp, while popping five caffeine pills a day and sometimes snorting ephedrine. He planted more trees than anyone else.

He did admit to me, once, that he was sometimes scared at how fast his heart was beating, during the workdays.

Five hundred milligrams of caffeine, on top of the dehydration and the hunger, and the pressure and the constant competition — I wouldn't blame him if it wasn't fun.

But he made a lot of money, that season, which was the only thing that anyone was trying to do.

And that's not only in the planting camp, of course — I mean, people everywhere are grasping at money. Lifetimes and lifetimes dedicated to the pursuit of it — so arguably it's a pretty good cause.

I was trying to make money, too. What else? I didn't argue with Ben about that. And the next morning we woke up in bed together — just accidentally, force of habit — and then we stopped speaking again.

42

When I asked Yukon to take me to the hospital, Maddie was in the truck with him. The F150 rolled up to my cache, and the window rolled down and and Yukon grinned at me:

I have Maddie with me, he said — She's heatfucked.

I peered through the sunlight into the shade of the cab, and saw her vaguely outlined: blonde head leaning back, eyelids down, fully limp. *Canada's Weather* was open on her lap.

It's pretty hot out, I said conversationally.

He smiled wider: Not in here —

Air conditioning.

I didn't mind the heat that day. I wasn't moving fast enough to really feel it. When I'd started planting in the morning, I'd been abruptly alerted that something was wrong. My leg was getting harder to ignore.

I couldn't move my ankle without feeling shooting pains. I was rocking on and off the heel, trying not to feel the front of my shin — but still, it was there.

In the morning I stopped and stood still. I thought about it. I didn't want to step forward again. It hurt.

I stepped forward softly. Onto the heel — more and more carefully. I perfected the rolling motion and I concentrated on moving fluidly and avoiding uneven ground, and I concentrated on not falling over. My two-step motion added a lilting accent.

Day 45, the land was black and white. The dead standing trees were charcoal skeletons, frail spines and spokes pointing up from between bright-white boulders. It was an eerie setting — it was like the flesh had been burned right off of the earth and left these knuckly bones exposed, gleaming whitely from below. The sun was bare but hazy in its own heat, and the matte-black earth was being cooked by it. Above the ground the air was dead windless, thick and heavy with expectation.

Early afternoon, I put one hand onto the door of Yukon's truck and I leaned on it. I squinted into the sun. I asked Yukon if he might take me to the hospital —

Not now, though — Like tonight after work,

And I explained it to him, a bit — I have this leg that's acting up, et cetera,

Then smiling less, his eyes glanced down at the shin.

I don't think I can bring you — he said — I think we have to work late tonight and I don't think I'm going into town.

He asked me: Have you talked to Konrad?

Mmm, I said, No, Haven't talked to Konrad.

He's your crew boss, He has to take you —

Yeah, Okay.

Yukon, not smiling at all, said — Look, I want to drive you tonight, because I don't want you to be hurt — But I really don't think I can today.

And he told me to stop planting if I thought it was serious. Don't be stupid, of course, it's not worth an injury, of course, I know.

You have your whole life ahead of you, Yukon said then, and he said:

You have Glory ahead of you; You can't have Glory if you break your leg.

And I smiled — Shoulda told me that two years ago.

You have your whole life ahead of you: Yukon could say things like that because he was maybe six years older than me, and because he was reasonable about these things, and he was thoughtful and he was careful. He made me wear a seatbelt when I rode in his truck.

Don't be stupid, he said and he looked down again — You're not even standing on it, he said.

I straightened the knee, centred myself over both legs.

Look, I said, I'm standing on it — I just want to get it checked.

A pause.

I want to take you tonight, but you have to ask Konrad instead.

And I said, Yeah, and I stepped back, and I bent down to pick up my planting bags — already full and ready. Yukon's tires kicked up dry dust, a sun-stricken cloud that hung glittering in the air as the truck roared away.

Konrad walked into my land a little while after that. I assume that Yukon sent him to find me.

I was rolling along, slow and mechanical. Around me, tight like a blanket, the air was humming with deerflies and shimmering with heat.

Konrad swaggered in towards me. Smiling crinkly-eyed Konrad, smiling, swarthy blonde and swaggering. I paused to look at him and then I planted another tree.

He asked me about my leg, and I planted another tree.

I think it's fucked, I said,

And he told I could stop if I needed to —

But then I'd just sit on the road all day, I said.

He smiled widely at that and shrugged, because he wanted me to keep planting, and of course I was going to keep planting.

Konrad said he'd take me to the hospital. Then he followed me around for a while, tugging on the trees as I planted them, checking that they were Good Quality Trees.

And I ignored him stubbornly for a while. To me, everything seemed pretty low and terrible, and the only witness there was Konrad — and I scowled and ignored him for that.

Konrad remained unaffected. That was his gift, really. My scowling had no effect on his inexorable smile, and finally I had to admit to myself that I liked having him follow me around. I liked not being alone, that day. And eventually and reluctantly, accidentally I smiled back at him.

When Konrad left he asked if I'd need Rodrigo to help me finish my land. And I nodded with relief, and said,

That would be great.

Orange hard hat, orange high-vis —

We could recognize our crew members from hundreds of metres away, by their gear and the way that they walked. Rodrigo was moving fast, pounding away, working towards me. We ignored each other, each going at our own pace, until we met in the middle. We stumbled into each other's trees and then we stumbled into each other.

We stopped to exchange words. Rodrigo was zoned out — he was in full-focus mode. When we met he stood up straight-backed and, all politeness, he asked me how the day was going.

I said the same things, like a summary —This leg, Y'know — and he nodded, et cetera, and I asked how his day was, too.

Very Good, he said. Nodded unsmiling.

Rodrigo was an actor — at least in spirit, if not in trade. He was always on one extreme or the other. On this particular day he was elevated and distant. Unsmiling, succinct.

I'm using a mantra, he said, Like you told me.

I had to think about that for a second —

What? I said, and he elaborated:

You said you used a mantra one day, Remember? Ten words over and over, and you had a Spiritual Epiphany.

And then I smiled — a delighted smile:

I did do that once! — and I told him, Great! How is it going?

He replied,

Great, It's going great.

He bent down and planted a tree. As he took his two steps away I asked him what it was —

Can you tell me your mantra?

He stood up straight again, eyes half-closed against the sunlight and said:

May All Sentient Beings Cease To Suffer.

He bent to plant another tree and I stood still and thought about that. By the time I answered he was two trees away with his back towards me and I don't think he heard me say,

That's really nice, Rodrigo.

May all sentient beings cease to suffer. That's really nice.

43

Konrad took Korry and Maddie to the hospital that evening after dinner, but he didn't take me. I'm not sure how exactly, but Yukon managed to finish work early, and we went into town together straight from the block.

More than an hour's drive to Timmins — It's okay, he said, I needed to get gas anyway — and we stopped for chips and Gatorade, of course, and we smoked and listened to good loud music, and we had everything we needed and a chance to talk —

Didn't talk about much, nothing important, just the kinds of things you talk about with someone you've known for a while, someone you already live with and work with anyway. Talked about people, and music, and mountains and all.

Yukon is a mountaineer. He works on mountains; he loves mountains —

I mean — truly — I think Yukon loves mountains as much as anyone has ever loved anything, anywhere, so sometimes we'd talk about that. Mountains and Glory — and he'd tell me, When are you coming to BC? When are we going to climb mountains?

Emergency room at the hospital: I was fresh off the block. I was clomping about in ragged grey steeltoes and these grey pants that were absolutely shredded at the bottom — they shredded nicely in strips, so once in a while I'd rip a piece off to use as filthy fancy-grade toilet paper —

And there was soot ground into my skin: hands to shoulders all blackened, and my face was streaked with stripes of sweat-soot mixture. The receptionist asked if I was working in the fires and I stumbled out some sun-slowed speech,

Like, Uh, Yeah? Re-planting … the fires? Like, planting … trees?

She looked at me and said,

So you plant trees and you come out looking like that?

And I smiled: Yep, yes.

She gave me a white handtowel and sent me into the bathroom to clean up. To me, this was glorious in sensation: hot-flowing clear water, temperature-controlled and endless from the faucet. Reverently I opened the taps, and then I leaned in and splashed my face with it, and then blood started pouring out of my nose. So I was leaning into the sink and splattering red all over the sterile porcelain, and simultaneously trying to clean up with this white towel, which was now spotted in dark-black-grey-red-pink, and I was snorting clods of blood out of one nostril down the drain —

Still it felt fresh and delightful.

I didn't know what to do with the towel afterwards. Really — I was standing in the little washroom with some toilet paper up one nostril, and I was looking at the once-white handtowel and thinking it through, when my name was called over the loudspeaker in the waiting room. So I snorted out some more blood and I exited the room, and hesitantly I brought the towel back to the receptionist and said,

Uh.

She raised her eyebrows, paused and said:

I guess I can throw that out for you —

Pinched it between thumb and forefinger, leaning away with her nose up, tossed it in a bin.

Then I started to laugh, accidentally, and the receptionist was looking at me again, raised her eyebrows again —

So I turned around and laughed silently while walking away.

On the crinkly paper on top of the hospital bed, I took my boot off and apologized:

I'm sorry, I haven't bathed in six days —

He moved my foot around, bent my knee, looked at the swelling, asked about the break.

This is what he told me:

If the bone was fractured again, you wouldn't be able to move your foot. The pain you feel now is residual soft-tissue disturbance, because you had a serious injury and that isn't going to go away. It's quite surprising that you can do this kind of work at all, on an injury like that. You'll have pain for the rest of your life and early-onset arthritis. But working on it won't make it worse, at this point. By all means, working on it is the best thing you can do to rehabilitate your leg. Keep working.

That's what I got. I smiled in response, Great, great, yeah, Great.

In the waiting room I met Yukon and he smiled when I told him.

See? he said — You're alright, It's all good, Everything's fine.

I half-smiled and half-scowled and felt sorry for myself and said,

I have early-onset arthritis and pain for the rest of my life.

And still he smiled, too knowing — these bush people don't let you feel sorry for yourself — and he put an arm around my shoulder and told me I'd be alright. We walked into the parking lot like that, and drove home under a smoky red sunset.

As that day ended, and I was stretching out horizontal in my bedding, I thought about the diagnosis and I started to be ecstatic again. The doctor had told me that nothing was wrong — that despite the daily pain and pain, I didn't have anything to worry about. I didn't have to think about anything; I didn't have to make any changes. All I had to do was ignore it, and I didn't have to worry about anything real.

And I was happy about that, as I lay down to sleep after the hospital visit — after the first hospital visit, I mean. Not the second, third, fourth, fifth, or sixth.

44

It's important to note that a tree planting camp could be a very happy place to live. Obscenely so —

It was anything but moderate. It could get pretty low, and then it'd get pretty high.

Once on Day Off, I was walking down a sidewalk in Timmins with the girls — with Korry, Hannah, Skobie, Megan — and I was brushing my teeth as we walked and spitting into roadside planter-boxes. Korry was wearing a high-visibility vest and a denim maternity skirt, with her fiery dreadlocks sculptured into some kind of octopus, and we were all walking to laundry, or coffee, or wherever it was that we went all the time,

And Korry said:

I think this is the happiest I've ever been in my life.

And I just looked at her and grinned, spat some toothpaste out, and I grinned hard because —

What a great thing to say, what a great thing to hear,

And none of us really answered her; we just kept walking along and smiling, everyone.

There was something about it, you know. The work, the lifestyle, the camp — As long as it was going the right way, it somehow started to negate all the malaise of the over-civilized:

Boredom, loneliness, insecurity, indecision, doubt and fear and self-loathing —

Most of these things would go away, for us, once we were spending every day out there working our asses off.

It was a simple, animalistic way of being, and it didn't require any abundance of thinking. At the end of the day, we just had these blind sensations and at the end of the day those sensations felt pretty good.

We'd get into the van, every evening when it was over. We'd squeeze in tight with the rest of the fifteen-member tribe — and everyone, abruptly, would be perfectly euphoric. Strangely, communally euphoric — at nothing but the thought of dinner, and sitting, and talking, and sleep — nothing but that, nothing else. I mean, what else is there?

As the season progressed, almost drawing to a close that summer, Arron and I would get in the van at the end of the day and look at each other and grin, shoulder-to-shoulder —

It was our last season, both of us. That was the last time. We just needed some quick money, and then it was time to get out into the world and start doing something real. You know, time to get serious, maybe think about a career. That's what people do after school, right? The next step is Career?

And at the end of every day, then, we'd start looking at each other and smiling and saying,

Hey, next season wouldn't be so bad, eh? How about one more season?

Sure, there was pain — and there were bugs and weather and thorns — and urgency and insanity and what-have-you —

And still, it felt good. It felt good at the end of the day. There was something about it — Something about being fit, fast, and free all at once —

The fresh air would get inside our heads, and everything became absurd, somehow. Everything became hilarious.

We'd go so long without seeing a billboard, without seeing an ad, a TV show, a magazine — It all seemed absurd when we got into town —

Like, Do people buy this shit? Do they believe it? Do people think this shit is real?

And we would laugh.

After my rookie season came to an end in Fredericton, the convoy drove us back, halfway across Canada again. Another two days in the van, with Tom driving, and with me always leaning on Ben. We dropped some of our crew in New Brunswick, then in Montreal, and we all parted ways in Ottawa. Only Ben and I headed back to Toronto together, on a coach bus. We were the last ones boarding, because it was all last-minute, and there were only two seats left: one at the front and one at the back.

I sat at the back, sat alone for the first time in three months, surrounded by humans who were all on a different pace and a different plane of living. Once while the bus was moving I stood up and walked to the front to talk to Ben. The bus driver looked at me in his rearview window and he told me to sit down —

You can't stand while the bus is moving, he said, You have to go back to your seat.

It was a shock. Truly, it was a shock — three months I'd gone without anyone telling me what to do.

Fresh off the convoy, I'd forgotten there were rules. I wasn't allowed to stand.

I looked at Ben. He looked at me. We didn't say anything. We didn't have to. I went to my seat and sat down. Alone and surrounded by people.

I kept a journal every year that I planted. In my rookie year, it was half-assed, not very committed. Still I wrote down my numbers each day, and I jotted down some notes.

And the last entry in my rookie journal, that year, was written when I arrived back in Toronto, back in the real world. The last entry was just a few words tight and messy, right in the centre of the page:

I don't want to be in the real world.

§ § § §

There's something about tree planting. There is a kind of romance — until it fades, of course.

You don't have to put up with any bullshit. You don't have to worry about yourself — about how you look, how you seem, about what you're supposed to be doing or how you're supposed to be acting — about What Might Happen — and you don't have to worry about the world. You don't have to listen to the news, you don't have to think about the future. You don't have to dress pretty, you don't have to make small-talk.

In exchange, you have to do a lot of really hard work, and if you look at it the right way, with enough practice, that can actually be pretty nice.

And maybe that says something about civilization, maybe — I mean, the fact that so many of us feel so great when we're no longer a part of it. But then, I won't claim to know much about that. In fact, I won't claim to know much at all, about anything. I won't have to think about it — any of it — as long as I just keep planting trees.

45

The tornado struck on Day 47, which was a half-day. It was an Actual Half-Day, which is a fairly elusive thing. Tom told us we'd be finished working at 1:30 so we could get to town early and really enjoy the Night Off.

It was stifling hot and I was working in a swamp, humid, and I was breathing water and bugs. The air was heavy with the buzzing and biting, the sky was pregnant dark overhead. There was a flooded moat I kept skipping across, stepping on black rolling logs to keep the swamp below my ankles. Muddy green land, wet like a jungle and impossibly deep.

I was alone and couldn't see anyone else, but I'm sure we all felt it coming, all at once. Just after noon, the sky closed to blackness and the air turned to thunder, and everything was anticipation — everything thick and rumbling, bubbling like it was almost at the boiling point. I finished what I was planting and went skipping back across the moat —

And suddenly the swamp was dancing around me and the air was all liquid, and the treeline disappeared behind this grey curtain —

Nothing but water all around: black-bubbling swampwater with the clouds right above it, and the raindrops falling so thick I couldn't see through them. Even the lightning flashes were revealing just greyness and blackness and mud.

At the road I picked up my gear — dropped my wet waterskin into the side of my wet planting bags, where the water was already pooling, felt the weight of the bags resting wet against the wet of my pants against the wet of my skin. I saw and felt and breathed just wet hot turbulent air.

Client truck drove up, spewing mud, and the young-girl-Client-quality-checker leaned out the window, told me,

There's lightning!

Because we aren't allowed to work in the lightning, only in the rain, and I stood straight and grinned at her wildly and I laughed and said, Yes!

She peered through the curtain of water and paused a second, awkward —

Get to the van, she said.

I laughed again and started to walk off. She went blaring in the other direction, leaning on the truck's horn, because the truck's horn means Come, to a planter, like a whistle to a dog.

The van was barely visible in the distance, parked on a hillside and facing outwards so Konrad could get us out of there, quick, and all the white-black turbulence around — shimmering walls made of water and flashes of light —

Planters were crawling out from the flooded landscapes on either side. Like tiny fluorescent insects, orange and green and white, like clockwork bugs swarming from the woodwork — and yet making so much noise —

Rodrigo, for sure, was the loudest, yelling taunts against the thunder — maniacal, frenzied cheering — and someone, another, was whooping in response.

Our Day-Off bags were piled on the roof of the van and getting soaked through and it was too late to do anything about that, and we tossed our muddy bags and shovels and gas jerries up on top of the backpacks and clothes and all the things up there. We congregated with maniacally grinning faces, everyone gleeful and shouting and not really saying much at all. We loaded in and squished against each other, slick and dripping, took off our shirts and sat skin-to-skin with puddles soaking into the stinking upholstery beneath us. The windows turned white with steam, so when I looked outside I could barely see; outside was a nondescript blur just fluctuating as it whirred past. The backseat was sauna-like in the dampness, heated with rain and skin, and we were breathing each other's sweat.

There was steam growing over the windshield and Konrad was ducking to try and see out underneath it, ducking to see out through the raindrops that were battering themselves on the glass. On our way out, Bennett's truck was sitting in the road and Konrad suddenly swerved, brought the van out to the left so two wheels drove off the shoulder. The van tilted, diagonal, and our bodies swung as a single mass, left. The wheels were churning fresh mud, drifting untethered in slippery wetness, fishtailing out of control. Rodrigo was whooping beside me and the van tilted, tilted, seemed to hang suspended — just briefly, and then the tires found traction. Back onto the road, everyone was yelling and cheering now, shouting and pounding on the seats, hot and half-naked and more soaked than damp, while the thick air was making the world invisible and we were all stuck together swerving madly through the mud. My left thigh was pressed against another planter's, and I could feel a heartbeat pounding hard against my skin, and I didnt know if it was mine or his.

46

We were the first crew to arrive at the fortress hotel and find sanctum there from the storm. Hannah and I took a room and waited for the girls — Krystal, Skobie, Megan — all absent. Arron joined us — his roommates missing, too — and we rotated showers and cracked beers and got some laundry ready, prepared to make moves, while the sky outside kept flashing on and off, opening and closing, and the streets were slick with creeks.

Two hours went by before they arrived, mud-bedraggled and soaked, stooped, silent.

Krystal told me the story about it, but later, after she'd showered, eaten, and smoked — when there were beers open and time to talk —

Krystal had tendonitis in her shovel wrist, then, and that was the first day she'd ever planted left-handed, and it was slow and painstaking and had made her feel like a rookie again.

So she'd been defeated by the day to begin with, before the storm even hit, and she was the first one back at the van when the day was winding down. Then she'd felt guilty about being early at the van so she climbed on top to load everyone's gear for them. She was hoisting shovels up onto the metal roof rack while the sky was flashing white, and suddenly she realized: (Holy Fuck) Lightning actually kills people — and with one planter left, dragging his feet towards the van, she jumped down and crammed inside.

By then Gabe was shouting at everyone to hurry, load up, because the roads were turning to soup in the rain. And as the van door slammed shut with fifteen people dripping inside he hit the gas and the wheels went spinning, and sank.

So they got out to push, and now the temperature was dropping, dropping fast after that heavy humid day,

And with everyone soaked through and Gabe yelling over the thunder they all pressed against the back doors, feet sliding, ankles getting suctioned in the mud with the rainwater running through it, and then the hail started to fall —

Dime-sized, said Krystal — Dimes clattering off their hard hats, bouncing off their shoulders and half-bent backs. Everything suddenly was freezing, turning whitish, with the sky still bellowing overhead.

They took turns huddling in the van, took turns pushing, five or seven pushing at once, and the wheels wouldn't find traction, even when they shoved logs underneath — and pushing, pushing — until Gabe called it off.

Parks arrived soon enough and hooked up a towline to his F250, so a group of planters left the van to push again and Parks hit the gas. The wheels of his truck, perched on top of the muddy track in front of the van — the wheels spun, and spun, and sank.

Everything freezing now and dripping: rainwater making glistening ribbons through the road, rainwater making biting streams over goosebumped skin — and that holy prospect of Day Off fading fast into a pipe dream.

B was called in, driving the school bus, and he waited on the better, drier road outside the block. Gabe sent the girls walking out first, and some of the rookie boys, and he kept the hardest veterans to keep pushing.

The last hope was Yukon's truck, and Yukon arrived and backed in to hook up the towline to Parks. And as he was backing in — before he even tried to pull forward — the truck bottomed out in mud, wheels not even touching solid ground.

That was the end of it. Almost two hours of pushing and spinning, then everyone cut their losses and walked away. High-stepping, yanking sodden boots out of the ankle-deep mud with every step. Silence apart from the rain and the thunder, and them all laden with Day-Off backpacks — clothes, phones, laptops — wet, very wet.

Bennett came for Parks and Yukon, left his truck at the entrance with the bus. The three deliverers walked out on their own behind the crew. Three of them each smoking a cigarette and saying nothing at all. Like three sore losers, Yukon said to me later.

I met Yukon at the laundromat that evening. 6 pm by then, and I'd long been indoors, and clean and dry.

I was sitting on a linoleum-plated table, legs dangling. I was wearing this denim thrift-store dress that I wore exclusively every day we spent in Timmins, which saved me the effort of buying or carrying more things. I was sipping a lukewarm beer and looking at the clunky TV monitor hung in the corner of the laundromat, high up between the beige walls and cobwebs. There was a red band scrolling along the bottom of the screen: TORNADO WARNING NORTHWEST OF TIMMINS. That's where we'd been working. Outside the streets were darker than twilight and the sky kept opening and closing — flashing and pouring on and off, abruptly, and the winds were mad.

When Yukon came in he asked if he could throw his laundry in with mine. It was a shirt and his only pair of pants. He'd bought new clothes at the thrift store just now, since all of his belongings were left in his truck, and what he'd been wearing was heavy with mud. And every week he bought new underwear and socks instead of washing them.

I said, Sorry, My laundry's already in the dryer,

And I said, Sorry to hear about your truck.

The deliverers more-or-less lived in their trucks; Yukon slept in his.

He told me:

I didn't want to drive in there at all, he said, But I couldn't be that asshole who left everyone else stuck in the mud — You can't just drive away, you know?

He shook his head, he took the beer that Arron gave him. He threw his laundry in with Arron's, and he went outside to smoke. I watched the tornado warning running below the news, over and over: all capitals, white words on red. I read the banner, and read the banner again, without looking at the news. I drank.

When the clothes were dry Megan and I slung them in bags over our shoulders to walk back to the fortress. The sky opened and came down on us, and all of our clean laundry started getting dalmation-coated with rain. We looked at each other — You wanna run?

We cracked our beers, and drank, and walked.

47

Krystal joined the Timmins camp the year that I was in Manitoba. She filled my place on Amo's crew. They told her that since she was replacing me, she would be held up to the same standards and expectations.

(These expectations had very little to do with trees and very much to do with Night Off infamy.)

She was nineteen then, and she was majoring in history at university while planning to become a schoolteacher. She didn't know anyone in the camp; she'd applied online and was one of the few to be chosen based on a resume rather than a recommendation.

In my third season, Krystal and I planted in the same camp, and afterwards she told me about her first impression of tree planters — of Tree Planters, as a species. By the time she told me this story, all of our six million trees had been planted; it was August, then, and we'd wound up in Megan's hometown, smalltown Ontario, and the three of us bought fifty-one beers between us and we hiked to a waterfall. I was wearing a cast on my left leg, at that point, and the cast got all scuffed up from clambering drunkenly around on rockfaces, and the three of us drank all day and all night and we finished the beers and that's where I was when I heard this story.

Day 1 as a rookie, Krystal met the crews in a parking lot in Timmins. There they were loaded onto two school buses and drove convoy-style to their first campsite, which was about four hours away.

Krystal was in the leading bus, and she was sitting quietly by while some obnoxious young Mexican-Canadian was causing a ruckus, demanding that Amo pull over so he could take a piss on the roadside. The rest of the crew and the driver were responding to the young man by shouting such things as

Shut the fuck up Rodrigo, and

Rodrigo get fucked

So Rodrigo scrounged up an empty Gatorade bottle, and politely facing the wall of the bus, he urinated in it. When the bottle was full he emptied it for re-use by chucking the contents out the window.

That was when he glanced back, down the road behind the bus, and he started to hoot and laugh like a madman, and grabbed the two-way radio from the dashboard and shouted into it, shouted at the bus behind them —

Yo, Tom, Did that water just hit your windshield?

The scratchy response came from Tom:

Negative, did not hit,

And Rodrigo madly cackled his reply —

Thank god, because it wasn't water, It was my *piss*!

A pause, and Tom drawled calmly (with that half-smirk, I imagine):

Amo, please prevent Rodrigo from using the radio in the future.

And young rookie Krystal, sitting quietly by, looked out the window and thought to herself,

Where the fuck am I right now?

They continued to drive, that afternoon, and the snow started to fall: thick white flakes drifting lazily in the grey breezes of early May. The snow continued to fall while they were setting up camp in the early evening — the same routine, clipping tent structures together and digging holes —

And then the snow continued to fall all night, and in the morning everyone woke up with their tents caved in under the weight of those thick white flakes.

And after that they were stranded in the campsite, with the road snowed in and no access in nor out, and evidently no chance to plant any trees — for four solid days.

The supervisor set up the dry tent's propane heater to blast warmth through the mess tent. After the first day the propane heater and the generator both failed, and then there was neither heat nor light.

Apparently it was so cold that many of the planters slept in their tents during the daytime, while the distant sun made for some kind of bearable warmth, and at night they gathered round a bonfire to drink until all the liquor was all gone, and still no access in nor out, and no power and nothing to do but play cards.

The cookshack was fueled by propane, so everyone was well fed.

Apparently spirits were quite high.

After four days the snow was melting and they all went to work, planting trees.

§ § § §

That was Krystal's introduction to the job.

Eventually, gradually, at some point, Krystal was no longer a bewildered teenaged rookie. She eventually became a wild animal who would arrive at the camp with almost nothing, eat every meal off of cardboard with her hands, pop caffeine pills and rage frenzied-like across the blocks. I once saw her plant trees in open-toed sandals, still flying with full urgency across fallen logs and brambles and swamp — matted hair, wide eyes, reckless abandonment. She became, at some point, a mad woman with an entourage of brother-like men who adored her.

48

After the tornado, this year —

Tornado Day, I remember, and I know it was Canada Day after that, and then things kind of go blending together. I woke up somewhere, woke up drunk and in the wrong place, went stumbling back to my hotel room, found the girls half-sleeping, half rustling and turning and mumbling things, something like 7 am.

I made noises at them, I turned the TV on, I opened a beer and went charging into the bed where Megan and Skobie were maybe asleep, but probably not asleep now. And maybe time went by and then Megan went rolling off the bed and tried to put contact lenses in, and she was missing one and came back laughing and swearing — I only have one contact lens, she said — Well go get the other one, I said, Put both in or you can't see — and she said, I can't, I only have one — Well, where's the other one? — It's gone somewhere — and we were laughing and she flopped onto the bed where I was lying with Skobie. We had a film playing on a computer on my lap, and

Megan was laughing because half of her world was blurry and I told her she just needed an eyepatch to clear it up — Do you have an eyepatch? she asked me — Of course I do — So first we tried a bandana and we wrapped it around her head, and the laptop was burning my thighs so I pushed it onto Skobie instead but the bandana wouldn't keep Megan's left eye closed and we were laughing about it again, and then we had another idea, and we put two bandaids taped over her blurry eye in an X to keep it shut, so only one eye was open and we were watching the movie for a while, but restless and rolling around and laughing over it.

Krystal and Hannah were in the other bed and just starting to move, Hannah first and Krystal still flat against the wall doing some sort of sleeping act. And, well — We have to leave soon, don't we? Don't we have to dial? We waited for the hotel to come yell at us, past checkout time, we lay flat and pushed the burning laptop at each other, still dressed in last night's clothes or underwear — and How nice would it be to shower right now, How nice would it be to feel fresh, but Who Cares — burning head and aching back and the bed felt so nice. We lay and finished the beers, lukewarm flat beers, breakfast beers, and — What if the hotel comes to kick us out before we're dialed? — Then tell 'em to get fucked, I said, Tell 'em to get Jackbooted —

Jackbooted means "violently and ruthlessly oppressive." We knew because Megan looked it up last night — but to us it just meant drunk — Get Jackbooted, Let's get Jackbooted tonight — And when the hotel tells us to leave, well, they can get Jackbooted, too. Except, this was the night when everyone in the east wing demanded refunds because we made too much noise, and we were in trouble then — We were too noisy, guys, We gotta shut the fuck up,

And we need to dial — Laundry needs to get dialed, Let's go get coff-ee-ee-coff-ee-ee needs to get dialed, Needs to, and somehow we packed up. Bags full and packed and dialed, all the dirty things packed in with the clean things, and the smell of us still lingering in that hotel room —

That smell that always followed us around: that block-smell, dirt and trees and bugspray and body odour. We packed our things and left our empty cans in the room and left our stench in the room and we wound up somewhere else.

Megan's eyepatch was gone, then, and she needed the drugstore for new contacts and we found Buldyke at the fast-food restaurant —

We ate shitty food, we bought fries and burgers and I inspected them, while Buldyke was flirting with the young-girl-Client-quality-checkers — And they weren't supposed to be there, you know — They weren't allowed to fraternize with us, but how can they help it when they're just our age, too, and we're way more fun and, What else is there to do in this city?

I inspected the fried potatoes, white and foamy identical prisms, and I said, I think french fries is a very disrespectful treatment of potatoes, and I laughed to myself. Meanwhile Megan was begging a drive to the drugstore and Buldyke was saying there was no room in his truck, and I was asking them all if they've ever considered the ethical implications of fast food, and I was laughing to myself and following them into the parking lot. Megan took the passenger seat so Hannah and I curled our way inside of the covered truck-bed where it smelled like the worst combination of old, old feet and decaying food and I leaned on something wet-ish and held my breath but couldn't quite hold it while laughing, and when we breathed fresh air again we were only three hundred metres from where we started, and we were in the drugstore parking lot, and trying to buy things —

Duct tape, they didn't have any duct tape, so I bought five hundred and twenty breathmints and we rolled off, three hundred metres again and saw a slope covered in dandelions.

I wanted to sit in the dandelions but couldn't remember how to speak and said, Let's go to the Yellow, and they understood me so we flopped down between the road and the parking lot and we ate mints. Hannah was picking the scabs off of her knees where they were infected: thorns, scabs, pus and bleeding — she looked up and laughed, What is my life right now? she said, My whole life is disgusting right now —

Time was rolling by and Day Off was getting done with, and we went staggering back towards the fortress, went inside the vans, still buzzing, and we rolled off,

Back to camp, we ate sandwiches we'd bought in town. The mints were all gone, and the sun was rolling off somewhere, and sleep was coming then, heavy hard dark sleep,

And at 6 am we woke to the sound of a truck horn blaring and we pulled ourselves upright and went off to plant trees.

49

Six days of thorns, after that, and on the sixth day I broke. My leg broke me, harder this time, and for the first time since my rookie year I stopped and cried.

We spent that week in a massive walk-in block, Day 49 to 54.

Every morning Konrad stopped the van on this plateau under a steep rocky hillside, above a sea of charred forest. We'd crawl out yawning, we'd don hard hats and backpacks and planting bags, and below us the standing matchsticks rolled in black waves forever, going bluish towards the horizon.

We'd walk up this steep hilly trail, up and down again over kilometres of exposed caprock, where once-upon-a-time there had been tree roots holding soil, holding a full ecosystem in place, and where now there was just bare rock. As it goes.

On either side of the trail, rolling boulders and thickets of thorns. It was chem-spray land made out of bristling bare sticks, the remnants of a meadow of raspberry bushes: shoulder-height finger-width sticks that were covered from base to tip with thorns, and tangled together in a ruthlessly abusive web, all around us and everywhere.

We'd walk in, maybe an hour to the back of the block, the furthest point from the road. Over the course of six days we worked our way back out, covering everything in spruce-that-might-survive, and all the while we were ducking and weaving and ripping ourselves open with the thorns.

The Five O'Clock Fuck occurred on most days around five o'clock.

One hour left in the workday, someone would yell the word FUCK somewhere in the distance. One at a time, like a wave rolling over the kilometres between us — one at a time, each planter would hear it coming from the plot of land beside him, and each planter would respond FU-U-U-U-U-U-U-U-U-U-U-U-U-U-UCK at the top of his lungs, and everything would cumulate into a roaring monosyllabic chorus over the entire block.

On a bad day, it could be somewhat spectacular.

We'd hear it, and then we'd yell FUCK, and then we'd know that it was five o'clock and someone, somewhere, had been having a bad day.

On Day 50, the yelling started early. It was maybe three in the afternoon.

It started with Rodrigo. In the real world, Rodrigo was a student of anthropology who spent his free time independently directing videos, blogs, and documentaries to post online. During the planting season, Rodrigo alternated between loud bursts of untethered mania and silent periods of thoughtful meditation. He would wake up earlier than anyone else and serve as an alarm clock by walking through a cluster of tents while giving out a weather report and an inspiring Quote of the Day. Everyone loved it.

Day 50 I heard Rodrigo yelling, though he was invisible to me. The only thing in my field of vision was thorns and thorns and the white sky above — and I kind of wanted to sit down and die there rather than taking another step forward. Rodrigo was pretty far away and I could only hear him because the thorns had shredded the cord of my earbuds so there was just this spitting noise in my ear until I turned it off.

What I made out from the yelling was a string of demented swearing and personalized gibberish. It went on for quite a while. As I was making my way out of the thornfields and back to the road — to load up more trees! — I climbed up onto a rocky outcropping and found that I'd completed a perfect square in a long-distance shouting match. Rodrigo's noises had been an inspiration, and now everyone was climbing up onto boulders to yell things at each other. I'm really not sure what this conversation was about — most certainly it was nothing at all but the excuse to make noises and to not be alone —

Travis and Ben had given up and moved into the same piece together, and they were standing high on a rock now, yelling at Brad who was across the road from them. A ways away from Brad was Rodrigo and his prodigiously-carrying voice, and across the road from Rodrigo was I, and we yelled at each other for a while, four corners of a noisemaking gibberish square, and eventually we ducked back in, submerged blind into the dull-brown torture chamber for another couple of hours and we all went ahead and planted more trees.

50

That day, Day 50, I told Konrad that it was the worst.

This is the worst, I said, This is just the fucking worst.

And he told me, Those are some strong words.

He was still smiling like he always was, like not a thing in the world had ever bothered him, like he found everything funny but not in a way that anyone else would understand,

And I gave up and half-smiled back and I said, Okay It's not *the* worst, but it's like pretty fucking bad.

At the end of the day Konrad hid under the tarp at my cache. He jumped out while I was standing alone there, emptying handfuls of dirt out of my planting bags, and I jumped and swore and threw dirt at him, and he said,

I was trying to cheer you up,

And he kept smiling, extra-smiling, because he thought it was funny like everything else.

I needed new earbuds after that, to fuel my music addiction — still the same twelve songs, yes, over and over again, and nothing else. Yukon went into town for gas after dinner and I went with him.

We went bumming around Walmart, wandering the shiny plastic aisles, dodging around the quiet slow-moving locals and avoiding the return to camp, and Yukon said, Do you need to buy anything else?

He saw pillows on the wall and said, Do you need to buy a backup pillow?

And I said, Fuck pillows, I don't even own one.

Yukon told me I would sleep better if I had a pillow, and I said,

Yeah, but if I slept better I wouldn't wake up in the middle of the night, And if I slept through the night then all of my waking hours would be spent planting trees.

Yukon told me that was the stupidest thing I'd ever said but I didn't buy a pillow. I slept with my head on a pair of jeans. I woke up in the middle of the night, in the middle of a dream about planting trees, and I delighted in the fact that I was lying in my tent and not planting trees.

51

On Day 51, it was the third day of the six-day shift. I dragged myself out of bed towards the mess tent and made myself smile by thinking that the day was almost over now, since I was already awake and dressed, and if the day was almost over then the week was almost over, and that meant Day Off was coming.

I passed Stefan in his navy bathrobe, while I was on my way to breakfast. I grinned at him and said,

Hey, Today is Hump Day and it's pretty much over already.

He smiled back and said,

That's exactly what I thought when I woke up this morning.

And we both continued walking.

52

On Day 52, a tire blew out on the way to the block, and we had no spare, so we spent about two hours waiting on the dirt track for the nearest van to bring us a tire.

Arron and I wandered into the black barcode at the roadside and took photographs of the trees. Mandog started climbing the trees. Jake and Harry started pushing the trees over. The trees were black and frail and dead.

Rodrigo took a video of Logan taking a shit in the bushes. Travis read part of a book. So did Ben.

Eventually we all sat down in a circle and propped up an empty Gatorade bottle in the dirt and threw rocks at it.

It was nice.

53

On Day 53, Tom told us that if anyone else brought a pair of moose antlers home from the block, they would be impaled with the antlers as punishment. Apparently Tom thought there were too many moose antlers in camp.

He also told us to toughen up. He gave an inspirational speech that went along these lines:

Alright, guys, we're getting towards the end of the season and I know everyone is hurting right now, but you can't keep taking days off just because you're hurting.

I've gone through entire contracts in the past without anyone going to the hospital,

And here, it seems like someone is going to the hospital every single day. It's getting ridiculous.

Look — I'm not saying that you can't go to the hospital if you're injured. I'm not saying that at all. If you're actually injured, then go and get it checked out. If you have an actual injury, obviously, you take time off. But having said that:

You need to know the difference between being hurt and being injured. Every single person in this camp is hurting right now, but that doesn't mean they're all taking days off. If you think you need to take a day off because you're hurting — think twice about that.

I know it's hard. I know this has been going on for a long time, and it always gets hard towards the end. Fuck, every day when you guys leave I go to my trailer and cry for an hour, and Ceilidh has to comfort me. Then by noon she's the one crying. (Tongue-in-cheek; the planters were laughing)

No, but seriously (he continued) I know that it's hard — and it's hardest of all for you guys — and I know you're all hurting — But we need to soldier on and get this thing done. I need you to be real warriors now.

And he had that crooked smile on at the end, so it was like he was making a joke — Warriors? How romantic —

But then, you know, we spent every day working ourselves half-to-death out there, and sometimes it was nice to feel like there was a cause. It was nice to feel as though it mattered. It was nice, once in a while, to be in it for the glory.

Warriors — that has a nice ring to it. Let's go with that.

54

On the following day I cried. It was unspectacular.

It was the sixth day of work, and pressure was mounting, and exhaustion was mounting, and we'd just spent the whole week in the sprawling walk-in Raspberry Block.

My crew — Konrad's crew — we'd finished our section of the Raspberry Block and we'd moved on to somewhere new. The new block was perfectly average. It was a clearcut, grey and choppy, with roadside access. It was bony and brittle but finally free of thorns.

We'd moved there at the very end of Day 53 and we'd celebrated. No raspberry bushes, no walk-in — it had been a relief.

Then on Day 54, there'd been a change of plans. Instead of moving to the Average Block, every single planter in the camp was going back to the Raspberry Block to help finish it. So with everyone working together, we were supposed to finish the land entirely, halfway through the day, and then head to town together for a glorious, glorious Night Off in Timmins, about which everyone was extremely excited since it had been six long days of work and two of our boys were going to be DJing at the club and everything was going to be disco-themed and spectacular.

So everyone in camp was going back to the Raspberry Block for the day — except for — for some reason — four of Konrad's planters. I don't know what the reasoning was behind this. I don't want to know. It was terrible.

I knew I'd be the first one kicked out of the van that morning. Sometimes you have a moment of clairvoyance three minutes before someone calls your name.

Konrad stopped the van and called my name smiling, smiling because it was a reward for something — Good Quality — Congratulations, you get to work in the Average Block today.

I said, *Whyy*, but he probably didn't hear me, because I was in the backseat, and then I opened the door behind me and climbed out of the sardine-tin and onto the ladder and threw my gear off the roof and climbed down and banged on the window to tell Konrad he could drive away now, which he did.

Being rewarded, as a tree planter, could be pretty terrible, depending on how you looked at it. If you were working in land that was better than everyone else's land, then it meant that your crew boss had done a favour for you, and you had to reciprocate that favour by performing, hard. It meant the highballers were gritting their teeth about it, and that everyone was kind of hating you, in a fleeting artifical manner, and it meant that you really had to perform really hard.

I planned to perform hard — I really, really did — and I guess that's what got me all fucked.

Cloudy windy dark grey day, slashy grey land, and no one around but the deerflies. Four of us were spread across that block. Hannah was just barely in sight of me, sometimes. Just sometimes, throughout the day, I could see her orange hard hat bobbing to the roadside, hundreds of metres away and outside of hearing range.

I know she was outside of hearing range because I asked her, later that night, if she'd heard me yelling all day, and she said that she'd only heard one word, once, which was the word FUCK, and she said it must have been very loud but she didn't hear anything else from me.

She said it cheered her up to hear me yelling the word FUCK from so far away, and I said, Good.

I pounded away in the morning, good high speed. I was ignoring the excess shooting pains like I'd been doing for weeks already.

The land wasn't that great. It was hard and bony. It was wood-chips and slash and it was hard to find soil. I was kicking a lot and being aggressive, one-leggedly. We were supposed to be done around 1:30; they told us the Raspberry Block could be finished by then. Every experienced planter knew not to rely on that; we all knew it was going to be a day of perfectly indefinite length.

Ignore the clock and keep working. And keep working harder.

Don't think.

Mid-morning Konrad visited me, leaned out the window of the van, told me that I had to plant eighteen bundles before 1:30. This was an ambitious goal in exchange for the favour he'd given me, and I said Okay. I was moving fast, and I was pretty focused and things were going alright.

Gradually there arrived the kind of pain that puts an end to it. It became clear, at some point, that something was not right.

But tell me this:

What is the difference between being hurt and being injured?

One tree at a time, with bolts of lightning shooting up and down my shin, ricocheting between the fracture scar and ankle. Holy shit, Holy fuck, I started to say out loud.

I didn't want to slow down. In any case, I wasn't being reckless: I'd been informed by a medical professional that I wasn't injured. I'd been informed by a medical professional that the best response was to continue working.

I pounded away, trying to not use my leg. Rocked onto the heel, rocked off the heel, without engaging any muscles, without leaning forward over the shin.

Fallen trees, logs, stumps. I moved to step over a blinding-white birch trunk, just over knee-high. I had to stop, carefully step, leaning on it for support, carefully rock over. It was obscene, frustrating. It was all contradictory to my profound sense of full-power urgency. I swore at the log — Oh, Fuck Off — Fuck *Off* —

This was a dark and frustrated place to be trapped in: trapped alone inside of a mind and a body, with nothing but a sense of urgency and an-almost-but-not-quite-crippling sensation of pain.

My blood was boiling with restlessness, and some dull uncertainty, corporeal confusion —

How do you know whether you are hurt or injured?

I slowed down, involuntarily. Something was definitely, certainly not going well.

They'd told me not to stop working. Doctor's orders. Nothing was wrong. Just chronic pain —

Just almost-but-not-quite-crippling pain for a lifetime.

But then, I had spent so many months — and not just me, but all of us — All of us had spent months-on-end training ourselves to understand one thing and one thing alone:

Do not stop moving, Do not stop moving,

Do not stop planting trees —

A branch brushed my shin and my leg went off like a siren and I yelled at the branch,

DON'T TOUCH MY FUCKING LEG

The deerflies were circling too tightly. I couldn't move fast enough to outrun them. Buzzing in fluctuating rounds about my head, landing on my shoulders, biting over and over again in the same spots. They were endless — fast and loud and endless — over and over again, that piquing, that same infuriating bite —

Two of them on my right shoulder, one after the other —

GET THE FUCK OFF OF ME

And I planted, too slowly, skin crawling, head reeling, shouting profanity, no one around —

No respite in sight, never, just trees and more trees, one day off and then more trees — and I'd already checked, and there was nothing wrong with my leg, just almost-but-not-quite-crippling pain — for a lifetime. Trees and trees and more trees, and how could I possibly be imagining this injury, and I cannot stop — I cannot possibly stop doing this — do not stop moving do not stop moving —

GET OFF OF MY FUCKING SHOULDERS YOU FUCK-ING MOTHERFUCKERS

Moving too slowly, momentum fizzling. Do not stop moving donotstopmoving —

My bags emptied, one tree at a time. I stumbled back out to the road. The power and energy and urgency were evapo-rating, fizzling out one tree at a time.

In the middle of the road, inside of a grey indifferent wind, I dropped my shovel. It made a tap and a *shckt* and a thump on the ground, and then it lay silent.

I leaned over my legs and looked at them: black leggings above ragged eight-inch steeltoes wrapped in peeling duct tape.

I closed both hands in a circle around the left leg, above the boot. I did the same thing with the right one, and then both, again.

The left was swollen, some three centimetres more in circumference than the right.

That was what got to me. That was all it took. I stayed bent, leaning forward over the gravel road, and the gravel went blurry and I felt saltwater balling up in the lashes of my eyelids and then it rolled off in drops onto the dirt. A few drops of water; five or six teardrops disappearing into the earth. I stayed bent over because if I'd stood up straight the tears would have left tracks in the dirt on my face.

I stayed bent over.

I waited a minute.

I picked up my shovel and walked back to the cache. Slowly. I picked up one bundle without bending my knees. Standing with one leg limp, I bagged up just one bundle, a half-load.

I walked back into the land.

I planted trees.

I didn't see anyone after that. Hours, planting, half-planting, half-loads, half-pace.

It was 1:30 eventually, and I had dared to hope, just barely. After that I put the hope away. Numbness was better. Numbness was much more productive than hope.

2 pm, 3 pm. Trees, hours, deerflies, minutes, steps and bolts of pain, and numb, quiet trees, and trees, and again.

At 3:30 I had planted exactly eighteen bundles. Exactly the number that Konrad had ordered from me, but two hours past the deadline. That was when the van came barreling in, triumphant and heavy with exuberant youth, blasting music — a mobile party-in-a-box. I was still wearing my planting bags when Konrad rolled up beside me, and I was ready to bag up again, because I didn't believe that it would end.

He got out of the van, said—Yeah the day's over, We wrapped, and he said:

You better have put in more than eighteen.

I glanced at him and away. Slowly, carefully spoke, felt my composure slipping, formed words most distinctly:

I Didn't. But. It Was Actually. Because Of My. Leg.

Konrad was looking at me and I ducked to avoid him, unclipped my bags and hooked them through the handle of my shovel, picked up my gear. My eyes were watery and I couldn't help it, and it had something to do with feeling generally pathetic, and the tinted side-windows of the van were staring right at me, and Konrad followed me while I walked to the ladder at the back.

Obviously there's something wrong, he said, So I can take you to the hospital tomorrow.

I climbed up, tossed my gear up. I held the ladder loosely, one hand. I held my voice tight and careful, and I tried to make it steady — facing away —

That would. Maybe. Be Good.

And all I could think while standing on the ladder was that the metal rungs were perfectly spaced to hit my shin if I leaned forward, right in the same exact spot that everything else seemed to hit my shin every time I did anything, and I half-closed my eyes and climbed down and walked away from Konrad around the right side of the van and he walked around the left side. I squished in, last seat, climbed past everyone with my head down eyes half-closed, inserted myself tight in the corner and leaned back and looked up at the ceiling.

Travis was beside me. He glanced at my face — a split-second too long — and then he looked back into *The Grapes of Wrath*.

I pulled my bandana down over my eyes, slumped limp and told myself, Get A Fucking Grip.

I said nothing to Travis and he said nothing to me and for that I was silently grateful.

And after that I got over it — eventually. I never cried about my leg again. Instead I started laughing, when they told me that it might be a bone infection — but then, I was also pretty drunk when that was happening.

55

Here's the secret:

I went tree planting three times, and I wasn't really in it for the money.

Is that obvious yet? There are a lot of ways to earn money, and probably a lot of them are less unpleasant than tree planting.

But I thought maybe there was more to it than money. I thought I could learn about something that, quite specifically, was not money.

I thought I'd discovered something real out there — something wild and uncontrollable and actually real —

And I wanted to get outside. Not just outdoors, but really outside —

Outside of the structures of control — outside of presuppositions and warring beliefs in entitlement — outside of houses built in identical rows and kilometre-long lineups of cars on the highway — straight lines and perfection-obsession — technology dependencies and professional facades — neurotic apprehension and this grinding machine, this overdeveloped closed-circuit system —

I just got claustrophobic and wanted to go outside, and I wanted to see what would happen out there — in a world that wasn't predictable, wasn't rigid, wasn't forced — a world that actually, for once, seemed like it was real.

And I've said already that I try not to get too romantic about tree planting. Of course.

It's a competition revolving around a money fetish and an ego trip. It's a lifestyle permeated by alcohol and drug abuse.

And it's a backlash culture, a counter-culture: the planting community doesn't exist outside of civilization, just underneath it, against it, or flitting around the edges —

But there it is, you know: Flitting around the edges of civilization, our little community is mostly invisible — and there's freedom in that.

It's mostly isolated — and there's solidarity in that.

And I grew up in a suburb and I'd been heading for adulthood while trapped between sharp-edged societal constrictions of imposed safety and imposed certainty, of the year-by-year instruction-manual life,

And everything that went with it — the beatification of consumerist idolatry and all the clinging emptiness of the superficial —

And all of that fucking inanity, or insanity, or what have you.

So here's what happened when I accidentally stumbled into tree planting:

It was the worst thing ever. Those days in the clearcuts, alone, exhausted and always on the verge of falling apart, day after day: it was shocking and yet, there was something in it —

I was a shitty tree planter to begin with. It was too hard for me. And because of that I couldn't let it go — not because of the money — but because there was something so real about it, so painfully and disgustingly real, and I wanted to know more about that.

The second time, when I went back, it was even more painful, but it was less difficult.

And it occured to me, entering my third season, that it might be possible to be happy while planting trees — I mean, to be happy while on the block, and not just in camp —

— to actually find enjoyment within that mundane, infuriating, endless task —

And it occured to me that if I could be happy while doing the least pleasant thing I'd ever encountered —

— if I could learn to be happy and calm in a clearcut, and through the pain and exhaustion and the infinite urgency of it all —

Then I could be happy and calm anywhere, doing anything,

And to hell with everything else.

Isn't that a great thought? Doesn't that make sense?

I started to get there. A few times, it worked. More and more, I was getting the hang of it, and I'd found a kind of peace in the motion of it, and in the sunlight (when there was sunlight) and in the wind (when there was wind), and I was pretty impervious to the rain and the bugs, and I could bear the solitude, quite well, and I'd started to move faster, I'd started to get the hang of it —

And when Stefan gave me a little bag of caffeine pills I figured I didn't need them, because it wasn't just about production, mindless urgent production —

It was about peace and freedom and fortitude, and that had nothing to do with pills.

I hit a hitch, after Day 54. I lost it after that. I didn't know what to do. When they said the injury might be serious, it became too real. I shouldn't have been there, when I thought it through — in the eyes of a real, civilized person — I could have just walked away. It wasn't worth the money — and if it had only been about money, about paperwork, then I could have just sat down and sued someone.

But it wasn't about that, and that's what made the difference. Yukon had been saying it for three years — Yukon, who couldn't live in a city because, he said, Everyone in the city is Afraid — and he'd been telling me for years: I'm only in it for the glory.

I was in it for the glory, too.

Until it got too real. It got inside of my head and I didn't know how to react —

How are you supposed to react?

What I learned, eventually, is that it doesn't matter how you're supposed to react. It doesn't matter what you're supposed to be doing. What actually matters is what you actually do, how you actually react.

You hit a breaking point, and either you break, or your limits break.

And if I learned anything while planting trees, it's that people don't break that easily — not permanently, at least.

56

After Day 54, my mantra was this:

I quit. I'm never planting another tree in my life.

First I told the girls — Hannah and Korry, the only two girls on my crew.

I told them I was done, and it was over. Maybe I was kind of joking, or at least I was kind of manic, so no one reacted to this announcement.

I'm quitting. I'm never planting another tree in my life.

I said that a lot, over the course of the next few days.

Didn't matter, in the end. I didn't quit.

We went back to camp before heading into town, Day 54. We'd left our Day-Off gear in the dry tent instead of on the vans, because the previous week everything had gotten soaked in the storm. The dry tent was generally flooded around the entrances, so we piled our bags together in the very centre of it.

Hannah stood on the roof and loaded our gear for us. My gear was a backpack and a plastic grocery bag filled with dirt-cheap lukewarm cans of beer. I hoisted my backpack up towards Hannah and put the beer-bag down on the gravel, and that was when a sharp little rock punctured one of the cans, and its skunky contents started pissing everywhere. So I took the offending can and stabbed the hole a little bit larger, cracked the can and poured the contents straight down my throat — and then I climbed over the backseat into the van.

And then — oh sweet lovely thing — I felt that skunky piss running straight into my bloodstream. Hunger, thirst, exhaustion, and a lightning-speed metabolism: like a dry sponge absorbing that beer. And so easily my angst was transforming — I felt the oncoming recklessness, the sweet-lovely abandonment of responsibility and reason, the warm caress of alcohol and feckless human stench, and all the excess and glory of a furious Night Off.

My memory ends around 8 pm that night, which is early even for me.

Apparently I missed a spectacular topless dance party at the club. I mean, I didn't miss it — I was there — but I really don't know anything about it.

57

My memory resumes around 10 am the following day. I was cracking a tall can in the hotel room with the girls. Megan, Hannah, Krystal, Skobie: all sprawled limply across the double beds, everything tangled up.

Skobie scolded me — That's my beer, she said,

And I told her, Okay, But I need it,

So I cracked it and drank it anyway.

I knew by then that I'd lost my wallet, though I hadn't searched for it, and though I had no clear memories about it at all. I just knew that I wouldn't find my wallet anywhere, because my driver's license and two bank cards were tucked neatly into my bra, which was the only thing I was wearing above the waist. And I didn't specifically remember taking those cards out of my wallet, but I knew that I'd only have done so if I was planning on losing the rest of my belongings. Which, of course, I had done quite successfully.

Hazy-brained, slack-mouthed, I told the girls:

I'm never planting another tree in my life.

The room was a mess.

Backpacks spilling their guts, and muddy boots and empty ziploc bags, food and shampoo and beer cans, and everything dusty-dirty-broken, everything clogged with that rancid block smell — that smell that's too big to fit comfortably indoors.

I'm never planting another tree in my life. I quit.

I rolled over on the bed and screamed into the mattress. A beastlike sound, it came up scratchy and muffled, an old horror movie sound effect. The girls laughed. Megan patted me on the back. I yelled into the bedding. Hard. I came up laughing. Megan cracked a beer.

I'm never planting another fucking tree in my life.

And so on.

I knew I was supposed to meet Konrad at 2 pm, because he was taking me to the hospital that day. The funny thing was that I couldn't remember us agreeing to meet at 2 pm.

I found him in the van, in the parking lot behind the fortress, and as we drove I asked him when we'd agreed to meet, and he looked at me and he was unsmiling.

A few hours ago, he said, We ate breakfast together.

I laughed.

Breakfast, I said, and I laughed about that to myself.

Konrad was driving. He looked away from the road, looked at me, eyebrows raised.

Are you kidding? he said, Do you remember breakfast today?

And I laughed.

That's great, I said, I'm glad I ate breakfast today, Good to know.

I laughed. Head light and spinning, everything felt unreal.

I'd lost my health insurance card, along with the rest of my wallet, but I figured that didn't matter. I figured I could deal with that later. I'd had the number on my health card memorized since I was fourteen.

Just in case of these exact circumstances, you know.

At the emergency room, we waited. It was a Monday afternoon and there were people all over the seats, soft people cleanly clothed — real people, husbands and wives and children screaming.

I didn't get out of the hospital until after 8 pm, and Konrad waited with me for most of it, and I was anxious about this because he was supposed to be driving the rest of the crew.

I told him: Konrad, Take them back to camp.

No.

One of the deliverers can pick me up later, Or Tom.

They might not be in town later, he said.

They'll come to get gas, I said.

They might not, he said.

(A pause)

Konrad they're going to be so mad.

(Nothing)

Brad and Rodrigo are going to yell at you.

(He shrugged)

Hours passed; we melted into the vinyl chairs, attached at the hips with tubular steel.

My skin was sweating rum and my hands were shaking. I leaned back in the chair and closed my eyes because I thought I might sleep, but when I closed my eyes my head went whirling — felt like a piece of trash bobbing in some stormy sea. I opened my eyes. I drummed my heels up and down against the tiles. I picked at the thorns stuck in my knuckles. I played with the surgical scar on my knee, opening and closing it like a mouth, until Konrad took my hand away and put it down on the chair beside me.

I rolled my head off the back of the chair and onto Konrad's shoulder, gazed in a glazed sort of way at the flatscreen TV, saw figures and colours moving back and forth, back and forth.

Hours passed, my eyes burned open, Konrad said nothing.

When I was moved into the next room, Konrad went to meet the boys at the theatre, and they yelled at him for being late. In the next room I was separated by a curtain from a fire-fighter — and though we were strangers, we immediately recognized each other: fellow bushpeople in arms — and we pulled back the curtain and talked about our jobs for a while, about our injuries, about our pasts, and about money and fires and trees.

Firefighter was in the hospital for a mysterious bad cough, persistent asthma, trouble with his lungs.

The doctor who looked at my leg took it more seriously than the last one had. She looked at it and said,

Oh, Yes, That's quite swollen.

It was worse, now. Much worse than it had been. It looked almost like the shin was bent in the middle, because of the lump growing out of the front of the tibia. All the skin was stretched tight and shiny around the fracture scar.

I had an x-ray done, and when the doctor came back she said she couldn't read it:

You didn't tell me there was so much hardware inside, she said,

And I laughed and said, Oh yeah, There is hardware inside.

She told me, It's hard to read anything on the x-ray when there's already so much going on,

And she went back into the hallway, and we heard her speak to someone else and say:

I have a very interesting x-ray for you to look at.

Firefighter glanced over at me, grinned and said —

I don't know if you should be concerned about that or flattered,

And I laughed.

When the doctor came back in she told me I was lucky.

Our Orthopedic Surgeon is in today, she said, And he usually isn't — But he's agreed to take a look at you — You're lucky.

58

So I went into a room with Orthopedic Surgeon and we had a great conversation. He asked me a lot of questions and I laughed a lot.

Orthopedic Surgeon was middle-aged and Middle Eastern with a round face, restrained mannerisms, and very sharp eyes. He spoke carefully with a strong accent, and he asked me how many trees I planted every day, and he said:

That's Amazing.

He asked me if I worked alone, and asked how many trees I'd planted to date, and asked where we camped, and every time I answered he said:

That's Amazing.

He asked me how I'd broken my leg and I said I was building furniture and he said,

Amazing.

I kept laughing and shaking my head and laughing, and my heart was suffering palpitations from the alcohol.

We went through the details. Compound fracture, twenty-one months ago. He asked me about the antibiotics I'd taken —

An IV, I said, For about one day.

How long did you take pills for, afterwards? Antibiotic pills?

None, not any.

He didn't react to anything I said, and I was never really sure whether he understood me at all — apart from when he was he quietly saying, Amazing, about things that seemed irrelevant.

He thumbed at the bone spur and I gritted my teeth and tried to express the sensation by telling him:

That. Feels. *Terrible.*

He said he could grind it off for me if I wanted, and I laughed because I was nomadically stationed in a work camp outside of reality and it seemed like a surgery just didn't fit into my schedule or budget, but thanks anyway.

He asked me if I was feeling tired. I laughed.

Do you ever feel nauseous? he said, Angry or depressed?

I didn't know how to answer these questions. It had been fifty-five days since I'd done anything besides sleep, eat, and plant trees as hard as I possibly could. I was tired and nauseous, and maybe I was unhappy, sure. But then, weren't we all? We were zombies, half-dead by the end of every day — or else ludicrously inebriated.

So I laughed and said, Um.

He asked me if I felt sick.

Yes, I said laughing, But that's probably the hangover.

He peered at me, asked — What?

I'm sick from alcohol, I told him and I grinned and then laughed.

He told me to watch carefully for these symptoms:

Fever, Nausea, Fatigue, Depression, General Malaise.

And I laughed and I looked at him like a question mark, because he didn't really seem to understand — I laughed sadly and said:

General Malaise.

When he told me I might have an infection in the bone, I said, Great, and I smiled at him.

This could be very serious, he said, and he told me that osteomyelitis can occur even years after the trauma.

And I said: Great.

He was also smiling and he didn't seem to mind that I was laughing all the time. He seemed amused, and I was amused by the fact that he seemed amused, and I said,

Well what the fuck am I supposed to do about it,

167

And I smiled to him.

I needed a bone scan and a gallium scan. They'd have done an MRI but the titanium in my leg prevented it.

I told him the contract was almost over, and I didn't know how long I'd be in Timmins — And how long does it take for these tests, and What am I actually supposed to do in the meantime?

You can either get the tests done here, or you can leave and get them done somewhere else.

And I laughed and shook my head.

What do I do now? I asked him — What do I do tomorrow?

He told me I could continue working. He said if it was a bone infection, the work would have no impact on it. He said this:

Your pain is not my concern right now. It doesn't matter to me if you are in pain while working. What I am concerned with is the bone infection, because if the bone is infected, it's very serious, and therefore you need to have these tests done.

What if it's a fracture? I said — Is it possible that it's a hairline fracture?

And he answered:

It might be a fracture — But you have a rod in your leg, so if it is fractured it won't go anywhere — Your leg is not going to snap again, he said and he smiled.

It won't get worse? I asked,

And he said, You have a rod in your leg.

He smiled, and I laughed, and I said:

So what do I do?

You have two options, he told me — You either get the tests done here, or you wait and do them somewhere else. Those are your two options.

I laughed:

What do I do?

How old are you? he asked me.

I had to think and replied slowly,

Twenty-one.

So, he said, You are old enough to decide for yourself, What you are going to do.

I laughed. The fluorescent lights were blindlingly white and I squinted against them. My heart was ringing like a gong and my skin was so hot it might have been giving off steam.

There was a pause, and then I said this:

Fuck.

Othopedic Surgeon was smiling with me, and then finally he laughed. Another short pause and he graciously filled my silence:

Okay, I will decide for you — I will try to book the tests within the next two weeks, and you will stay here and get the tests done before you leave.

Okay, And tomorrow? I go back to work — Tomorrow?

In twelve hours I would be on the block again. It was too soon. That was the thing I couldn't wrap my head around. What was I supposed to do when I got to the block again?

He told me:

I can give you a prescription for rest, if you want to rest tomorrow.

And I smiled again, and shook my head, again, and said —

If I rest, I don't make any money.

He nodded and he smiled back —

Exactly, So here is the problem: If you were a normal girl, I would tell you to sit down, put your leg up, maybe use crutches for a while — But you are not a normal girl, so if you want to work, you can work — That's up to you.

And I laughed. In the course of a single conversation, this medical professional had determined that I was not normal. I laughed —

And that was the verdict I received:

I would continue working and I would wait on appointments and wait on results and I would continue planting trees.

I was supposed to leave a phone number at the hospital, so that the hospital could phone me, so that I could book the appointments — but I didn't have a phone number. At the time, I just didn't have any use for a phone, and I didn't have very much money, either, so I just didn't own a phone. I had no contact information that I could give to the receptionist.

8 pm, I found Konrad in the parking lot. Half the crew was still stuck in town and waiting on him, waiting on me. I took Tom's phone number from Konrad and gave it to the hospital, because Tom was really the only one who might have cell reception during the day, and because Tom would know my schedule better than I did, anyway, so I gave them Tom's number and kind of assumed he'd answer the phone and make an appointment for me, which he did not actually do, in the end, but that was really my only course of action at that point, so that's what I did.

And then I told Konrad the diagnosis, and I laid down in the back of the van and was hungry and thirsty and aching and just barely sober and I watched the ceiling as we drove back to camp and I could feel the rattling of the road inside of my leg.

Yeah, and that's when it started to get kind of serious for me.

59

In the four different contracts that I worked, I knew one planter who didn't drink on Nights Off.

He was a guru, our fifteen-year veteran in Manitoba. He was a thinker and an artist; he spent the off-seasons working on independent films in Toronto. While planting, he was indefatigable and unreadable and imperturbable. A compact man, always clean-shaven, I couldn't tell his age but he seemed young enough.

On the day that I arrived he introduced himself as Dan, said he'd been working the contract long enough to answer any questions I had about the quality standards and the land. He was soft-spoken and approachable and somehow — despite the setting — he struck me as a gentleman. In camp he spent his evenings writing, and on Day Off he rented a room by himself, to rest and to work. I felt like he'd found some kind of enlightenment in all of it.

On my first Night Off in Manitoba, Dan came out with us for a few beers, which was an unusual event. That night the cops came and broke up the party and we hid in a freight car on the tracks behind the motel. Two planters were meanwhile taken in and fined for public drunkenness, and another spent the night at the station undergoing a Mental Health Assessment because he made a joke about suicide and because his arms were all cut up from the bushes.

That day, it had been pouring rain. In the morning, my eyelids had swollen almost-shut from the blackfly bites and I could only see properly when I was looking at the ground. Across the road from me a rookie had been smearing swamp-muck across his face as a shield from the bugs. We were drenched through completely — everything was soaked. There was no choice, no relief, nowhere to hide from it, and it was hard to get drunk that night because we all felt feverish and weird, and we thought maybe it was from all the bug-spray, or else from being soaking wet all day.

We tried to get drunk anyway. Then the cops arrived and a few of us slipped quietly into a greasy unlit traincar.

I sat on the floor with Dan and discussed French films of the 1970s. Two weeks earlier I'd been a student in Paris.

We leaned against the dusty wall of the freight car, sipped on beers in a civilized manner, ducked away from law-enforcement flashlight beams and exchanged notes on Eustache and Godard.

That was the only time that Dan came out for Night Off with us. The rest of the time he was silent and sober and planting trees at a terrifying pace, like a robot on fast-forward.

On that same day — my first Night Off in Manitoba — many of my friends were meanwhile experiencing the least pleasant workday of their lives, one province to the east.

I've heard accounts of this day from several different people, and they have all independently told me that it was unforgettable.

The whole week had been swelteringly hot and everyone was wearing as little as possible, wearing just t-shirts and leggings, and still they were sweating and burning under the hot high-summer sun.

Then unexpectedly, as the vehicles were arriving at the block on the 7th of July, the temperature dropped to almost freezing, and freezing rain fell from the sky unceasingly for the rest of the day, and everyone continued to work through it while wearing almost nothing and slowly feeling their extremities go numb.

The problem is that there's no escape from freezing wet rain — not out there.

No matter how fast you try to move, the icy water will not feel good. With every step it will be there, and it will claw through your clothing and your skin, and it will rip you open to gnaw on your bones.

The problem is that you want to stop and you want to hide, but there's nowhere to hide and it only gets worse if you stop. The only thing you can do is keep moving because there's nowhere to go — and you know there's six, eight, ten hours ahead and you clench your teeth and give up your right hand. Abandon your right hand completely, because it can serve its purpose just fine as a claw frozen tight around the handle of your shovel. Your left hand is in the ground with its red-white fingers frozen straight, and you find that the ugly icy mud feels warmer than your blood. You put your head down and give up your shoulders to the wind and give up your feet to the swamp. And maybe you cry but no one will see because you're alone, completely alone, and the tears blend in anyway because your cheeks are clad in rain, and maybe you cry and maybe you swear and maybe you sink into some dark hole that you never wanted to know anything about — but you sure as fuck don't stop moving.

That's the only thing — That's exactly what we know for sure:

Do not stop moving — Do not stop planting trees — Do not —

It becomes easier with time; it's hard on the rookies at first.

That day, that July 7th, B was in his fifth year of planting. He told me that he didn't stop moving. He told me he didn't take a sip of water or a bite of food all day. He told me that it was terrible and that the money was very good.

Jake was in his second year of planting and he didn't stop moving either. Every time he planted beside a standing tree he prayed that it would fall on him so that it would end. Nothing fell on him and he continued planting all day.

Travis was a rookie then and he sat down on a stump and he says he lost his soul that day. Konrad arrived to try and motivate him, and Travis said, Get out. Konrad got out. Brad and Travis — both rookies — met at the cache, trembling with bloodshot eyes betraying tears, and each saw their misery mirrored by the other and neither of them had anything to hide.

173

Megan was a rookie and she also sat down on a stump and she says she lost her mind that day. She couldn't move any of her fingers and she was laughing. She was speaking to herself out loud in muddled gibberish for several hours and she was laughing hysterically at the sound of her own voice. When she sat down on a stump she made a deal with herself to become a better person as long as she made it through the day.

The crew bosses were trying to help. If the planters wanted to stop, they could go into the vehicles and warm up for an hour. Most of the planters didn't want to stop — or couldn't stop — you can't just stop —

But Management called it off at 5 pm instead of 6 that day.

Tom was one of the crew bosses, then. He was the only crew boss who reacted by donning his old planting bags and getting out of the bus. One at a time he met each of his planters, and he went into the land and planted a bundle alongside each of them, one at a time, outside in the pouring freezing rain.

When I asked Rodrigo about it, a year later, Rodrigo said that there had been nothing but suffering that day, all day long. He said that he tried to think his way through it, and tried to Embrace The Pain — and still, no matter what, there'd been nothing but suffering — until the end of the day.

Then, he told me, when the day was finally over there was something else entirely. When the pain ended there was something else, something that was high and insane and contagious —

Everyone made it back to camp and they were all in love with each other. There was that giddiness and that soaring relief, and that priceless sense of unity —

Because they'd all been alone, but they'd all been in it together.

60

That was July 7 of the previous year.

By coincidence — completely inconsequential coincidence — it was also July 7, this year, when I bent over my leg and cried on the roadside.

The evening that followed, I told Yukon about it, and he responded like this:

Hey, We're all in this together.

And I half-smiled and said:

That's what they say yeah,

And I climbed out of his truck and closed the door.

It was the nicest thing he could have said. I guess it was the right thing to say. And still it didn't change the fact that no one was in it with me, this time around. I couldn't think of anything to change the fact that I was going to be alone all day, with this limb that kept screaming, and suddenly — for the first time — it wasn't a game anymore. This wouldn't be over, for me, at the end of the workday. And this thing wasn't real to anyone else —

This time around, there was no one in it with me.

There had been one afternoon, just prior to that, when I was working with B's crew instead of my own. Konrad's planters had been told to re-plant a block because of Quality issues. There were four of us whose trees didn't have any Quality issues, so four of us had been moved to continue planting elsewhere.

That afternoon, B was bombing around on a quad, sharp and business-oriented, managing more planters than usual. He stopped at my cache twice. The first time was to share some friendly banter; the second time was to incite some friendly competition. The second time, when he pulled up, he told me pointedly that Megan was planting more trees than I was.

I smiled, replied —

Give me a break, I'm crippled,

And he rolled his eyes and said flatly:

There is nothing wrong with your leg.

Outwardly, I think I laughed and I said:

Well.

And I bent down to plant a tree —

While inwardly, I flinched.

I bent down to plant another one, and the quad roared off.

And what I learned, that afternoon, was this:

I was in it alone.

There was no one else feeling what I was feeling, this time around.

Okay, so I was in it alone.

Okay.

61

After I'd met with the Orthopedic Surgeon, I had to ask Tom to book appointments for me. We rolled back to camp and found Tom leaning on the back of his pickup with one of the crew bosses, and they were talking and laughing aloud as they always were. Konrad came with me; I walked up to Tom and told him I'd been to the hospital, and I was half-smiling and full-hungover, and I said,

I just found out I'm pretty much dying.

Tom didn't react to anything I said. To be fair, he didn't generally react to anything that anyone said. I eventually developed a theory that you could tell how closely Tom was listening, based on how little he appeared to be listening.

He asked me two questions afterwards, and both times without looking at me. He was standing with one hand in the pocket of his jeans, and looking out across the gravel pit and speaking in the same slow-rambling tone as he always did. First, he asked about what causes a bone infection, and then I realized that his main concern was the liability issue of a serious injury occuring in the camp. And then I felt bad about this and said:

No, It has nothing to do with tree planting. If it is a bone infection, it's because I didn't finish my course of antibiotics when I broke my leg in the first place — I was supposed to stay in the hospital for forty-eight hours and instead I left after twenty-four hours because I didn't like it there.

(This was true. When my roommates had come to visit me on the day after my surgery, I'd simply fled with them.)

Tom glanced at me and repeated, You were supposed to be on antibiotics and you just left.

Well, I said, Yeah, So that might have been a bad idea.

I summarized my conversation with the surgeon by telling Tom:

Pretty much if I come down with a fever, I'm dying.

And Tom asked his second question, looking casually at the horizon:

So, when you say you're dying — How likely is it that you are actually going to die?

Oh, I said — I think I'm exaggerating about that, Sorry.

Konrad spoke then:

It's really serious, though, My dad just had a bone infection in his hip and he had to have multiple surgeries and couldn't walk for a really long time.

And I said, Konrad —

Konrad looked at me and said,

You won't be able to walk, You might have to get the bone replaced, It's really serious.

Tom spoke again, slowly, told me:

I would be more comfortable with you not dying.

And I said —

That's how I feel about it, too.

Good, he said, At least we're on the same page.

62

The skin infections were getting pretty serious, then.

Korry had gone to the hospital on Day 45 and she'd been prescribed antibiotics, and she was taking those every day, and still applying topical cream under the gauze and duct tape in the mornings, and the infection was still there.

Buldyke and Andreas and Bennett were taking antibiotics for theirs, too.

Mandog never had anything prescribed for the one on his forearm — never went to the hospital — and neither did Rodrigo for the one on his wrist. They squeezed them out, wiped clean the yellowy-white paste, covered them with duct tape, and repeated that process when necessary.

Bennett's infection was on his knee, and he was taking antibiotics, and the first infection was almost gone, healed, when the second one appeared and started to grow.

There were more, too, throughout the camp. These infections were becoming somewhat common, and everyone had seen them, but there was nothing to be done except get the prescription filled and maybe pad it with gauze and with duct tape and carry on, carry on.

And in the end, as it turned out, it didn't matter very much — who took antibiotics and who didn't — because, as it turned out, the infections were caused by Methicillin-resistant *Staphylococcus aureus*, which is a staph bacteria that's developed a resistance to the typical antibiotic treatments, and which is also extremely contagious — and which is especially contagious among people who are living in close quarters, and especially in insalubrious conditions — and which can also develop into sepsis with a fatality rate of 20% to 50%, and which is evidently a Fairly Serious Thing.

People kept going to the hospital and getting these things looked at. But despite the frequency of hospital visits, no one actually received the diagnosis of MRSA until after the season was already over — and so everyone continued to plant trees, pop infections, pop antibiotic pills, et cetera, until the season was done —

Except for Bennett, who was hospitalized for four days and operated on and forced to leave the camp —

And apart from that small hitch, things carried on as per usual.

And it was hard for anyone to complain about anything, really, when everyone seemed to be suffering, in some form or another,

And, still, despite all of that, spirits were very high.

We were having a lot of fun, actually. Actually, I didn't even want to leave. Ever.

63

I was camped at the top of a little incline at the edge of the gravel plain, under the trees there where the forest began. I'd kicked and scraped out a flat portion among the rocks and brambles up high so that my bed wouldn't flood when the heavy storms came, as my rookie tent had flooded before. Hannah and Megan had camped on the flat ground below me.

After I talked to Tom about the hospital visit, Day 55, I went back to our triad of tents. Hannah was sitting in the gravel, there, fixing her boots by wrapping them with duct tape, because the soles had ripped off in various places, and because there were only two weeks or so left in the contract, and who wants to spend a day's pay on new boots at a time like that —

Hannah and I grinned at our reunion as though it had been days — it felt like it had been days — and I went ahead and told her my story, but I was just absolutely ranting by then. I was grinning and cursing and spewing out nonsense — and as I ranted Megan unzipped the door of her tent and crawled out. She was wearing pyjamas and a hoodie, sucking on a beer can, and we started laughing riotously as soon as we saw each other.

Darkness fell with the three of us lounging about in the dirt and passing a can around and —

Shit, fuck, shit we have to work tomorrow, fucking hell —

Laughing about that and forcing ourselves to bed —

Of course, as it goes, we never wanted to go to bed. As soon as you go to bed, then you have to wake up and plant trees again.

I didn't want to do it anymore.

I didn't want to leave the camp, but neither did I want to wake up and plant trees.

That night felt wrong to me. That night everything was moving too fast and in the wrong direction — and I was too messed up to wrap my head around it. Six hard days of work, and I'd spent my day off in the hospital, and still I had nothing in the way of a diagnosis, not even an appointment, never mind a solution, and the next day there was nothing to be done except to plant trees all day, every day for another how-many-days — and it wasn't going to be any less painful.

I was nauseous and aching and laughing about it, and I was trying to find a best-case scenario, and I couldn't think of one. The possible outcomes were, firstly, a bone infection, which by all accounts was serious —

Or secondly, a fracture, which would only get worse as long as I was still working —

Or maybe — as I'd been told once or twice — maybe nothing was wrong with it, at all — which just meant that it wasn't going to go away, ever, at all.

And regardless of any scenario, there was nothing for it but to plant trees — all day, all the time — because we weren't paid to calm down and relax. We weren't paid to sit down and think it through —

And it was evening then and there was nothing for it but to go to sleep and wake up at 6 am and go to a clearcut and plant trees —

For a couple hundred bucks and so much pain —

And, no, I never considered leaving the camp,

And I didn't want to but I knew that I would bend over and plant trees the next day —

And the day after that, bend over and plant trees,

And so on,

Indefinitely —

64

When the van entered the block the next morning, I was tandem-sleeping with Korry. My shoulder was behind hers and our heads were leaning against each other, with her dreadlocks padding our skulls from knocking, and both of us were asleep like that.

Exhaustion reigned over everything. I woke up gently and didn't move because my body was heavy-limp against the seat, and my eyelids were welded shut, and I could have stayed like that for two more days and been content.

I was deeply underwater when Konrad called my name and I dragged my eyelids apart, barely, and — wow, what a powerful undertow, an almost physical sense of dread — and the only thing to do was numbly move.

I used my muscles like remote-control machinery to climb out of the van and up the ladder and then back down. Numbness gloved my hands while they tore at the iceblock tree pods; numbness padded my knees against the stones on the roadside. Numbness held the weight of the trees as it settled onto my shoulders and hips and onto my knees and my godforsaken shins.

I found myself numbly under the drizzling rain, with the sun masked like it was underwater, and I started to move. I bent over to plant —

A tree, and a tree, and another.

My face felt burning and I thought distantly of fever, and I thought about:

Fever, Nausea, Fatigue, Depression,

and General Malaise —

And it wasn't very difficult to feel any of those things, at a time like that.

I stumbled around at a rueful pace, and intently I paid attention to the feelings in my left leg, and I found that those feelings weren't very pleasant, and all I could think was that it was a cruel joke to say the words *General Malaise* to a tree planter.

And there was a long, slow day ahead of me —

But, you know, I realized something new from the first tree that morning:

Planting was a relief.

I found it — that day. I found peace in the motion of it, and respite and familiarity, and I sank gratefully into the rhythm. Despite that nagging pain and the dreadfully dragging pace of it, I discovered quite unexpectedly that it felt better to be moving than to be standing still. It felt better to be doing than to be dreading.

So I moved.

And the dread dissipated, draggingly dissolved, and so did another dull day.

65

Motivation was something that the crew bosses tried to cultivate. In a way it was part of their job. The crew bosses were paid based on a percentage of what their crew earned; their wages depended on our production.

So every crew boss had to be able to manage their planters, but a really good crew boss was able to motivate them, too.

The motivation could come in a lot of different forms — but it was very rarely a gentle voice of encouragement. The thing is, if the motivation was really going to be effective, it meant that the impetus to Plant More Trees had to outweigh everything else. The numbers had to be (or had to seem to be) more important than the exhaustion and the discomfort. The numbers had to outweigh everything.

Often enough, the motivation came as a strategic application of pressure, tested from all different angles until one of them worked. Sometimes it was about competition and ego; sometimes it was about glory and achievement; sometimes guilt and shame; sometimes loyalty and respect. Or, depending on the planter, maybe it was just about money.

In any case, in some form or another, the numbers were supposed to outweigh everything else.

On Day 59 Konrad tried to apply a bit of pressure across the board. The land was going to be good, apparently: it was burn land, clear and sandy for the most part, and Konrad told us to take advantage of it.

He told us that we were pushing for an all-crew Personal Best. A PB Day! he told us. Everyone PB!

Which is something we heard often enough. Management liked to say these things, to apply pressure, like:

Take advantage of this land. You might not see land like this again. Today is the day. This is where you make your money. You have no excuse to not PB today. Don't be fucking around in there. You make excuses, you're fucking yourself over. Man up and get your fucking head in the game.

Konrad didn't really try it with me, and to be fair I don't really blame him for that. I think all of my crew bosses learned that no matter what they said to me, the response would be half of a smile, possibly the word Great, and otherwise total disregard. I wasn't trying to be difficult, but generally that's just how it was.

Konrad didn't try to push me towards a PB on Day 59, nor on any of the following days. In fact he took the opposite approach, and he simply wrote me off.

Which was reasonable, really; it was truly reasonable given my performances of late, and my circumstances too —

Still it was somewhat unpleasant.

Day 59 — PB Day —

Creamy sandy land, he'd said. The pressure was on.

I watched most of the crew being cut in — highballers first. Ben and Arron were working across the road from each other, matched for competition, each sprinting headfirst into those wide open burns.

We continued down the road with planters disembarking into the greyness usually two at a time, usually paired off to race.

Before he called my name, Konrad braked and looked out the window and deliberated for a second and looked at his map. I looked out the window, too, and I decided we were no longer on the block.

In the rearview mirror above the windshield, Konrad and I made eye contact as he called on me. Obediently I climbed out and we stood shoulder-to-shoulder in front of the van while he pointed me in:

Go that way, diagonally, until you hit older trees and then work left,

And I looked at the flood, the ground made out of black water between barricades of charred branches, where he was motioning me in. Looked at it and donned my daily numbness and said to my boss,

Oh Fuck Off.

Konrad had turned to walk away and now he turned back with his smile still on and said —

What?

Because he hadn't heard me.

So I said to him carefully:

Konrad I fucking hate you.

And he smiled, and he put one hand on my shoulder and said,

I know,

And then he walked away, and left me alone.

66

Plodding, early afternoon.

I was distracted by the sensations in my leg and by the burning of my forehead and by the depressing nature of everything and everything, and so on and so forth,

And I kept taking two steps and bending down and putting a tree in the ground and stomping at it, and then doing that again,

Again,

And I started to think about what it was that I was doing,

And I thought about that for a while, while plodding onwards over this wood-chippy swamp-front lot in the bushes,

For a while,
And the way those thoughts all concluded was like this:
Nothing is making this worth it.

Then instead of taking another step forward I didn't.

I leaned on my shovel and stood bent-backed out of habit.

I thought about moving forward, in an absent kind of way, and I couldn't find a reason to do so, and so I stood there for a while and then after a while I sat down.

On the ground beside a stump I sat without unclipping my bags, legs bent and the left one gently folded on top. I put both hands on the earth, hands dirty but dry, thick and scarred leather-knuckled hands.

I looked at the earth. It was thick and scarred and ugly too.

I let numbness have my mind and I let a minute pass by.

A great many minutes passed by.

I took the music away from my ear. There was the breeze and the calling of crickets and the buzzing of flies. There was the sun against my dirt-textured arms and the sun soaking into my leggings. There was one leg throbbing slightly, but pleasantly at rest.

I sat still for an hour. Unplugged robot, a pile of faulty machinery.

I unclipped my bags and stood up out of them, left them lying there with the buckle open, and my shovel flat beside them.

Thoughts flatlined — irrelevant undercurrent behind the buzzing wind and flies.

Meandered away between the spiky bush-branches, across the black-bullrush swamp, and found myself on the road. I sat down there, too, and I drank water and ate an apple, and looked at the bundles of trees in their white plastic straightjackets, and sat cross-legged on a slight incline and looked at the gravel road, watched the tires of the van roll over the gravel road, and watched Konrad's boots come out onto the gravel road,

One boot at a time, swinging forward one boot at a time.

Konrad was working hard; he was setting his crew up for PB Day. He tossed bundles out of the van onto the ground beside me and I watched him.

How long have you been sitting on the road, said his voice.

And I made my voice say:

Forever.

I noticed him trying to be stern with me:

You have two minutes to get back in your land.

I turned my face, up, towards his face.

I watched his blue eyes looking straight into mine for half of a second, and then his eyes flicked away, and his face turned away, and his boots moved back into the van and the wheels went rolling off,

And I stayed sitting.

Another half hour maybe. I started to be restless again — mentally, emotionally restless, never physically — and still there were four or five hours to go.

So what, then?

I took two caffeine pills and one cough drop and three ibuprofen.

I stood up and floated back into the spiky dark bush. I found my bags half-full and loyally waiting. I strapped them on and I planted more trees.

And that day ended, too, as days tend to, and the crew didn't hit the number that Konrad had aimed for, and it didn't seem to matter either way.

67

At dinner Megan asked me about it: How's the leg?

And I told her smiling: I'm dying from General Malaise,

Then I laughed and said, I guess we all are,

And suddenly I recognized that statement as an adequate summary of the entire condition of all life and existence.

I grinned at Megan with sheer delight, and she grinned back and said,

General Malaise,

Which was exactly the same way that I'd responded to the Surgeon,

So we laughed about that for a while.

68

When we lived at the Campground, we would sometimes cross the highway after dinner and go for a swim.

We'd only go if there was really time — if there was an early finish or an in-camp Night Off — because on days when we were home after 8 pm, all we did was eat a meal and go to sleep again.

When we went to swim, someone would usually drive. Usually it was a planter who had their own vehicle in camp, because usually Management was still working after dinner — Management was more-or-less working, usually always — so we'd load up into the back of a truck or the trunk of a hatchback, and we'd cross the highway with our bare feet dangling out in the wind over the rolling asphalt,

And those moments were really nice.

The Campground was an RV park with a sandy beach and a deep cold lake and a convenience store, all of which were novelties for us. The people there in their trailers and motorhomes would watch us swimming and they would smile and wave at us and sometimes wander over to talk. Meanwhile we would be stripping to underwear and shouting at each other and diving under the water to feel the mud-sweat-stickiness usurped by fresh freezing cold. On special occasions we would even use soap and shampoo.

On one occasion I rolled over to the campsite in the back of Buldyke's truck along with the assistant cook, Vanessa. She told me that sometimes, on a really good day, she and Ceilidh would come to the Campground on their afternoon break.

The two of them had to wake up at 4 am every day, to prepare breakfast for us, and then clean up after we left and soon enough start on dinner. They had to have the dinner prepared by the time we got back from work — these huge and heavy meals for sixty-or-so superhuman appetites — and then they had to stay up afterwards and clean up again while we slept.

Their only break was the empty afternoon between breakfast clean-up and dinner prep, and generally they'd use this break to nap, since they didn't get to sleep very much.

They lived almost entirely alone, with each other, in this clearing in the bush, for the full 71 days and then some, and they worked every day almost without cease. They spent our Days Off procuring massive quantities of food and supplies to prepare for the week ahead.

So Vanessa told me that on a really good day, weather permitting, they'd spend an hour or two at the beach at the Campground in the early afternoon. She told me it was weird and surreal, to escape from the barren windy gravel pit, and walk twenty minutes, and encounter this —

A bunch of obese people seated in the sun and doing absolutely nothing all day.

They don't even go swimming, she said, They actually just lie around, And then I go back to camp, and the planters come home, and everyone looks anorexic and falls asleep standing up —

Two completely different worlds, she said. Right across the highway.

69

Following Day 59, we all woke up around 2 am because of this crazy storm.

I heard it and stirred to consciousness and the first thing that came to my mind was:

Please let it be 6 am right now, Please let it be so stormy that we can't go to work —

Like any Canadian child praying for a Snow Day, every morning before school all the way through the winter.

But it was too early in the night and I knew the storm would be over by morning and we'd be working again no matter what. So, okay, I lay flat on my back swathed in fleece and nylon, and I fluffed up the rolled-sweater under my head and lay still to enjoy the spectacle. A full-body experience, much better than cinema —

My paper-thin roof was raving wildly, flapping and dodging and collapsing in towards me and then billowing out. The floor of the tent, right beside me, kept lifting and punching about and it was held down just by a couple bags, clothes and gear —

And I thought that my tent might well enough lift and go rolling down the little incline, and I thought that would be pretty inconvenient, I mean really inconvenient but not really deadly —

Meanwhile the raindrops were just tearing themselves to shreds against the membrane above me and thunder was rending the air — monstrous — and lightning kept making eerie blinding scenes out of the blue fabric bubble that encased me. Kept lighting up and lingering in my eyes after everything went black again.

But the most surreal thing was this odd sense of telepathy about it. It had something to do with that time of night, when dreams and darkness start to blend —

There was this knowledge that all of us — sixty of us — were all certainly awake and all experiencing the same thing, the same time, like sharing the same dream. All of us lying flat on our backs and isolated in these tiny thin-membraned cells and all of us just barely dry and barely safe from it — watching and hearing like one entity scattered through sixty sets of ears and eyes.

I thought probably someone's tent was going to give out. I imagined someone going rolling across the gravel encased in a nylon-metal tumbleweed, and I considered peeking out to see, but it wasn't worth it —

And I really had to pee but that definitely, definitely wasn't worth it.

And we lay awake and listened for an hour, maybe, maybe more, and lay happily enthralled with the flashing black-and-white and the heartless shredding symphony,

And floated gently into unconsciousness as the thunder slowed, the rain became a lullaby,

And we woke up again at 6 am, to a flood and a large collective giddiness and a long wet workday ahead.

70

The flat expanse of the Campground was a miniature system of bodies of water after the storm. There were foggy creeks making tracks over the gravel, flowing into ponds between the trailers, under the tents. The mess tent was flooded ankle-deep at the two entrances, and all the little holes in the tarp were feeding waterfalls into yellowy insect-spotted puddles on the tables and chairs.

The cooks wore rainboots and splashed through the pond at the back door to set the breakfast tables, and most of the planters wore boots of some kind, too, and splashed around, too, and everything was damp but otherwise normal, and people were grinning and exchanging notes, like —

I had to hold my tent-poles up with my arms straight out, like this for an hour, because every time I let go it kept collapsing on me —

I realized how much I loved my tent last night — It was the only thing keeping me dry — And I was like, Way to go, Tent, I love you —

Or conversely,

Yeah I woke up with my head in a puddle!

Everyone grinning and joking and so on.

By that point five days had passed since I'd visited the hospital, and I still had no appointments booked, and I still was finding it corrosive to my state of mind. Telephone tag had ensued between Tom and the Department of Nuclear Medicine after I'd given them his number. Messages were left by each party, and eventually they shared one conversation in which it was established that Tom didn't have the information required to make appointments on my behalf, and nothing at all was decided.

And so, Day 60, despite the push to finish the contract, despite all the pressure and prospective glory-or-shame — despite the fact that you can't just stop planting trees —

I gave up and stopped planting trees, for a day.

I found Tom in the morning. He was standing outside of the mess tent beside a rainwater-pool, eating cereal out of a bowl with a notebook tucked under one arm.

I told him:

Okay, I think I need to make these appointments, because, I think I need to; And maybe I need to go in person or it won't happen,

And Tom nodded slowly while looking in a different direction and he said,

If you want to go to the hospital, this wouldn't be the worst day to do it,

Because apparently the latest shipment of trees was still frozen and it wouldn't be a full day of work — and on top of that Tom was already taking John to the hospital because John had a rock lodged into the side of his eyeball — and therefore I could tag along and maybe it wouldn't be the worst kind of inconvenience to anyone.

Which was a relief to me. It was a soaring relief, and I prepared everything as if I was going to the block anyway, and dressed for it just in case we ended up there afterwards — you never know —

We didn't end up on the block. Tom made the offer to us after we'd finished at the hospital. It was late morning and he said, Do you want me to try and get you guys to the block for the last couple hours?

And John said, Not really, Half of my face is still frozen and my left eye is blurry.

And I said something like I couldn't care less, and the block wasn't close by, so we didn't end up there.

John was Ben's younger brother; he was a teenaged rookie that year. He planted the same way that Ben did, more or less. Apparently these things run in the family.

John didn't say very much. He sat in the backseat of the F350 that day while we drove around to the sound of Tom's honky-tonk tunes. Conversation was at a minimum. At one point I turned around and asked John,

How did you get a rock in your eye?

He looked at me, paused, and responded:

I was planting trees.

At which point the conversation ended.

Tom was running errands in town after the hospital visits. We had the camp's blue drinking-water barrels, empty in the bed of the truck, and Tom filled them up at the fire station with a fire hose running out of the garage.

He also went to the drugstore to pick up prescriptions, and that was when I went in and bought myself a bottle of extra-strength caffeine pills. Back in the cab of the truck, John said:

I could have just given you some of mine, I have like five hundred.

And Tom asked him —

So Ben's got you on the caffeine pills already?

John shrugged Yeah, to which Tom answered:

What an idiot.

And this was more-or-less a joke, since Tom and Ben were actually good friends —

But I'd have probably said the same thing.

It's like this: dehydration and anxiety are two things that you don't need to augment, when you are out in the clearcuts all day. Both of those things are available in massive quantities, without adding the side-effects of caffeine to the mix.

On top of that, personally, I'd never wanted a dependency; I'd never wanted to need a fix.

But, as I've said, after a certain point you no longer give a fuck.

Day 60, my dilemma was this:

The Department of Nuclear Medicine had booked me in for three appointments to determine the cause of the pain in my leg. I was to have a bone scan on Day 64, a gallium injection on Day 70, and a gallium scan on Day 72. Then I would know — maybe. Another twelve days of waiting, and then I would maybe know for sure, maybe.

And when I asked Tom what his guess was, regarding the end-date for the contract, he said that the last day should be Day 70.

Which meant that I would be planting for ten more days, and the pain wouldn't be any less, and there would be no peace of mind —

But it was only ten days. I would survive ten days. And simply there was nothing to do, in the meantime, but plant more trees.

Which meant that it was time to stop worrying about it. So I did.

And eventually I stopped worrying about anything whatsoever, because there was nothing I could do either way. There was nothing I could do except get hard and get numb and get over it.

And plant more trees, of course. So I did.

71

The next morning when Konrad called my name, Mandog and I were the only ones left in the van. Mandog looked out the window, at the land where I was being sent in, and he raised his eyebrows and said:

Does Konrad hate you?

And I said Yes, and I climbed out and took my extra-strength caffeine and my extra-strength painkillers and I went in.

Day 61: again, the sixth straight workday (for everyone but John and I) and it was the last day of the shift. We had to finish the land that day before we could head into town, so it was a Wrap Day Half Day. There was the potential for us to finish in the early afternoon, as long as everything went smoothly, but then nothing ever really went smoothly, and instead it all culminated in a nonsense-style improvisation-finale that dragged long and dragged on.

We were mixed up with Gabe's crew that day, and all thirty of us ended up wandering around, converging and diverging, meandering down roadsides and mashing around in swamps, and half the trees still seemed to be frozen, and everyone was burning out their caffeine,

And around 2 pm someone heard over the radio that the rookie crew was already out and headed into town —

Oh — Fuck — gnashing teeth and snarling vets —

And we were there for another two-and-a-half-hours, though we didn't know at the time —

(No deadline meant it could be infinite)

And no one had eaten any food for a long time, since it had to be Pounded Out —

Faster — we're Wrapping any second now —

And everything faded blankly into numbness and urgency,

Not many jokes being exchanged anymore, Just put your head down, Keep your eyes open,

We can stop once it's over —

And eventually it was over — eventually —

And, suddenly, as it goes — everything was suddenly good.

It was over. It was good. We crowded into the van. People were smiling. We'd made good money, too.

We could laugh and joke again, all of a sudden, and then we went barrelling straight into town.

72

Our crew went out for a real dinner that night. We took the time to go to an actual sit-down restaurant. We sat on the patio, which was otherwise empty because of a cold wind, and we smoked and joked and made a real time of it.

Rodrigo and Arron and I were exchanging important discourse on past events, and reliving old lives that we'd somehow forgotten in all of this — Can you imagine we used to be like that? — as though it all happened to a different person — and pitchers and pitchers of beer —

The poor waitress had to serve fifteen people who couldn't act right, couldn't keep a straight face about anything. Fifteen people being loudly alien — not really drunk or obnoxious, but just acting like no one ever acts in public, and dressed like it too —

The hunger made it hard to sit still, and also hard to think, like we couldn't look at anything — couldn't focus on anything — couldn't really hold up a conversation — and none of it seemed remotely important anyway —

When the food came — unbelievable, some kind of record-breaking moment — Waitress came back out after five minutes to check, How Is Everything? And all the plates were already wiped clean, and we were asking each other,

Should we get another meal here? Do we have time to wait for another one to come?

Debating for a while —

It's too expensive, And we have to get drunk now,

So we got the bills and left, and went to the fast food joint and ate our second meal there instead.

73

So, it can be hard, at the end of a planting season, can be really hard to readjust.

Yeah.

You wind up revving like an engine in neutral. All this momentum and nothing to do — and still that hunger and that thirst and that reckless vulgarity — and suddenly you're alone and people around you are all moving too slowly and they're all calm and secure and you can't quite explain to them —

At the end of the season, it's like one of those old cartoons: some character runs and runs straight off the edge of a cliff and doesn't even notice. You know, they run for a moment through the air and don't fall until they look down —

Somehow it feels like that. You keep running and running, and when you finally stop and look around, you realize you that you can't fall asleep without getting drunk, and you've really got nothing going for you in the real world, and no one around you has any idea what you're talking about, in general,

Or maybe that's just me.

For months afterwards, every single time I found myself in a bar — anywhere, any province, any country — I had to compulsively scan every face just in case there was a tree planter there. It only took a drink or two before I'd be looking around for them — just in case, serindipitously — in case there was someone there, to really drink with. I mean, someone who would understand, someone who would know.

74

Day 61 was our final Night Off in town. The last one.

It's hazy but we wound up all in a circle at the club after they tried to kick us out. They tried to turn the lights on — Okay, night's over, guys, Get out —

And instead Tom commandeered the DJ booth and started playing his Bob Dylan, Neil Young, The Band,

And everyone wound up in a circle, clasped together and swaying, moving in and out and singing or mumbling along. Linked together arms-across-shoulders, everyone floating around like one kind of living thing, breathing and rocking and leaning on each other. A weird cultish slow-dance, it wasn't particularly exciting and it wasn't sexual at all but it was somehow romantic and warm and it just kept going. Three, four, five songs and still everyone was just swaying about on the dance floor and smiling and holding on —

In the morning Hannah told me she didn't give a fuck about anything. That's how it started, I think.

The five of us girls, again, woke up tangled up across the beds and stirred simultaneously to consciousness and started saying things, whatever things, any things,

And eventually Hannah said, like a revelation:

Hey, guys, I don't give a fuck about anything,

Grinning and she said,

This is amazing — I just don't give a fuck about anything, at all, no matter what, I don't give a fuck.

So I told her:

Fuckless — That's the word for it — When you have no fucks to give, you're Fuckless.

And Hannah said,

This is amazing — What if I sober up and I'm still completely Fuckless? What if I'm just Fuckless forever?

Well then you're set for life, I guess.

Imagine never giving a fuck about anything, ever again.

Megan was moving slowly around the room and picking up all the beer cans that were littered about — on the bedside table, on the bureau by the TV, on the bathroom counter, on the window sill. She was picking up each can and pouring all the remnants into her water bottle.

She filled up the full one-litre bottle with flat warm beer, and she drank it a few hours later. Later, when we were lounging on the sticky linoleum floor of the laundromat, leaning against the aluminum window frame with the dirt in its grooves, and we were laughing and we didn't want to leave the planting camp.

It was my last year, you know. I was never going back after that. This is the last time, I kept saying. And every morning when I filled my damp cold bags with sodden trees, with three hundred heavy iceblock seedling trees, I told myself again: It's the last time, This is the last time, And I am never coming back.

Then Megan was there saying: Look, my degree is useless and there's no way I'm ever paying off my student debt without doing this — (Megan was a student of history and philosophy) — And just imagine trying to get a real job — Imagine —

And why don't we just keep planting trees and go drifting through education all winter, and wind up with a Ph.D. and a million trees planted and never even deal with any of the shit that goes on in the real world — Why not, Why not, eh?

75

Back at the camp, all of the Management trucks were missing. Always working, every Day Off.

Tom, Yukon, Parks, Bennett: they were off unloading the next reefer. Bennett was there with them despite the fact that he'd just flipped his truck into a ditch. He wasn't hospitalized until much later in the evening. Tom didn't sleep all night. But we didn't know that then.

We were getting ready to go to bed. Filling up water bottles, making small talk. We heard rumours of an eight-day shift then. Eight straight days of work to finish the contract, and we'd be done on Day 70. And I realized that I'd be stuck alone in Timmins, then, waiting on my final appointment, and everyone else would be done and gone, and I started to miss everyone already.

Eight more days, eight days only. Nothing for it but to plant more trees. Pop pills and plant trees, and so on, and unless my leg gave out or a fever burned straight through me, I would plant trees. Eight days only.

76

It was lucky for Bennett that he flipped his truck over. It was almost certainly a good thing — in the long run.

It was Bennett's first year as a deliverer, now; his fourth year in the bush. He'd brought along his girlfriend, Jess, as a rookie that year. Bennett and Jess together epitomized cool: they were two beautiful people who never raised their voices over anything. The money they were earning, that season, was going towards a four-month skiing tour of Japan.

On that Night Off, Day 61, Bennett hadn't come to the club. He'd gone to town early in the day to refill a prescription for anitbiotics, because there was a second infection now blossoming redly on his knee. Apparently he'd felt poorly that day — tired and ill and generally malaised — and he'd taken his antibiotics and gone to sleep instead of drinking.

The following day, Day Off, while Megan and I were sprawled on the laundromat floor sipping pisslike plasticky beer, Bennett was transporting a quad to the new block.

He had the quad strapped onto the bed of his F150 and he was driving alone down a logging road, towards the block where Konrad's crew would be working the next day. It was a narrow winding road and it was busy with other trucks. Bennett was calling his kilometres over the radio, which was the standard procedure for preventing collisions. Calling kilometres allowed the drivers to be aware of other vehicles on the road, as soon as they were within range. Bennett was hearing responses through the radio — but barely. The speaker was crackling and spitting out some broken-up backwoods Quebecois, which was incomprehensible to him.

So that was why, despite his use of the radio, Bennett was taken by surprise when he crested a hill and found himself face-to-face with a haul truck —

A hundred metres away, fully loaded and barrelling straight at him.

Bennett slowed and steered his F150 out to the right. He figured the road would be wide enough to pass comfortably, so when the right wheels started to dip slightly he was just annoyed at the thought that the truck might get stuck and Parks would have to pull him out.

And that's all he was thinking until the wheels dipped under, everything went flying, glass was shattering and the curtain airbags went off,

And then he was hanging upside down by his seatbelt, and the windows were all shrouded in green bush.

Bennett was pretty shaken by this — physically — serious adrenaline.

He radioed the trucker, who pulled over and came to help him out, and they climbed out of the ditch and made some conversation in questionable Quebecois, and they agreed that the truck was quite precariously perched in that leafy gully and it really wasn't a good idea to do anything about it, right now, when it might just roll again.

The trucker moved off and Bennett waited a while, waited shaken and alone and empty-handed, and eventually he hitched a ride with a passing hunter; it was just ten kilometres up the road to where Parks was working. From there they called Tom and started to get everything sorted out. There would be paperwork and technicalities and the truck still needed to be recovered from the ditch —

But still the blocks needed to be prepared for the next day, because the next day the planters needed to be pounding, at the pace of the Push-to-Finish (eight days left) — and so the work carried on and Bennett remained on the block with them, although Tom had him sit out on the sidelines while the rest of the team kept going — moving the trees, unloading the reefer, setting up caches — Parks and Yukon and Tom, along with Bennett sitting by.

Meanwhile, on the slope of that leafy gully, most of Bennett's belongings remained stranded in the inverted cab of the F150. Same as Yukon, he'd more-or-less been living in his truck.

So, inaccessible, now:

Wallet, cell phone, laptop, clean laundry, a broken case of beer, the block maps and work papers and the quad, and also his recently-filled prescription of antibiotics.

As the day wore on, Bennett started to miss the antibiotics more than anything else, because his knee was quite definitely swollen and throbbing and leaking and extremely tender to touch.

He was limping before the end of that day. He was feeling sick and hot and certainly malaised.

Bennett started to mention it to Tom, that he was going to need more pills — really, not kidding at all — that he really wouldn't be able to work the full week without getting another prescription sorted out.

So that was the reason why, that evening, Tom drove Bennett to an after-hours clinic — just to procure a new bottle of pills —

And that was when the doctor looked over Bennett's knee,

And at the red hot swelling that now stretched from his ankle to mid-thigh,

And measured his fever at 101 degrees,

And told him with a great deal of urgency: that the possibility of a blood infection was very, very serious now —

(That being sepsis, of couse, with a 20% to 50% fatality rate in MRSA patients.)

And sent him to the hospital then, immediately, where he was taken by professionals and placed in a bed and hooked up to an IV.

And Bennett said, afterwards, that if he hadn't lost the pills he would have pushed through everything instead of revisiting the clinic. Which is why, maybe, he was lucky to have flipped into a ditch on Day 62.

77

Tom told us all, transparently, that Bennett had flipped his truck and that he was in the hospital for something unrelated. This was the morning meeting on Day 63.

After the meeting we crowded into our vehicles as always, four separate crews, and we prepared to be on our way.

Fourteen of us were shoved into the van, and Tom leaned in over the driver's seat to give us a pep talk. This was a special, novel occasion, of course — a crew-specific pep talk from the supervisor himself.

What he told us went something like this:

Today you'll be in the best land you've seen all season.

Which, of course, we'd all heard before. It was like a Management cliche: The best land of your lives!!!

Tom told us we were all going to have great days and there were going to be PBs today and, he said,

You're the highballer crew, but you're dragging down Quality right now. If you don't plant one-hundred-percent perfect trees today, we're pulling you out of there — Because we don't have time, this late in the season, to work on Quality — So you are all going to have huge days today — There will be PBs — But they have to be one-hundred-percent perfect trees, every single one.

And he said some encouraging things, I'm sure, and then stepped back and was replaced with Konrad. Konrad climbed in and turned back to face us, and he said nothing — he just gave us a sweeping meaningful gaze, and then he started to drive.

Brad, sitting beside me, said:

Well, fuck, There goes my day.

And I'd thought the same thing.

The pressure alone was enough to be crippling, sometimes.

I took a bunch of caffeine that day, but it didn't really work that way. I mean, you can't just take a bunch of pills and expect them to do the work for you. Your head has to be in it, too. And depending on who you are, your heart has to be in it, too.

I went flailing around in the land, fighting everything and trying really to push, because Tom had said so — not just Konrad, you see, but Tom himself — but the caffeine wasn't really enough to compensate for the pain and the difficulty.

It had all been untrue, anyway — that old Management cliche. As it turned out, Management had really only looked at the outside of the block. Bennett's quad had never made it there, evidently, and the vans weren't able to get past this massive ditch at the entrance —

So we all walked in that day. We walked in a docile herd, shuffling quietly and peering intently through the rain to pass our judgments on the land. To begin with it was beautiful; it was enough to shut us up completely —

Straight sandy furrows, long and open, glinting almost metallically beneath that knifelike mist.

We made our way along, up and down in the flooding mud, on and along towards the back —

And then, there it was again. There was the greenness springing up after the burn, there were the bushes to fight through and the flooding and thorns and Does it ever end?

I went tripping around in there getting all fast on caffeine, running with that empty churning motion, and collapsing on my left side once in a while —

And actually, technically, I did hit a PB that day,

Although when Konrad asked me about it I just snarled at him,

Because, well, what a low desperate state to discover inside your own head.

78

I was working very much alone that day. I could see Korry in the distance, sometimes. Way down along the quad-track, I could just barely see her hard hat as a floating lime-green speck, bobbing about — and apart from that I was alone.

But then when I came out of my land in the mid-afternoon, staggering lowly through the grey drizzle and up to the cache, there was Ben standing there.

He wasn't doing anything. He wasn't planting trees. He wasn't even wearing planting bags.

What are you doing here, I said — not unfriendly, but like a genuine question, because it didn't make sense — and I folded to my knees and ripped open a slippery white bundle. I had no idea where Ben had come from, or where his land was — maybe he was working close by, somewhere, but I hadn't seen him all day.

And in answer to my question, he said this:

I can't plant another fucking tree.

And he sat down on the dirt track, maybe two metres away from me. He sat down with his ankles crossed and his elbows around his knees and started talking, talking that sounded like pacing, like someone pacing inside of a cage —

I can't fucking go in there. This is — Fuck — Every day is a competition. I can't get out of it. I can't take a day off from it.

Every fucking day I'm competing with every single person in the camp — I can't go in there without having to think about Arron, Jake, Andreas — I have to keep up with every single one of them every fucking day —

He was looking at me, but he wasn't really looking at me. He was talking too quickly. I opened another bundle, absently moved handfuls of floppy stems — and Ben told me:

Jake was the highballer last year and he said he didn't want to do it again, this year — He said it was too much pressure, and I thought that was ridiculous — I mean, fuck, of course I want to do it — Of course it's fucking great, I'm making more money than everyone else — But I get it now — what Jake said — I mean it's fucking insane, it's driving me insane and I can't plant another fucking tree.

Kind of shrugged, vibrating always, full of words overlapping.

I looked up and nodded, and said, Yeah I know —

Because, yes, I know, and I would have said more, but what?

The caffeine makes it worse, he said — It makes it really, really bad.

I know, I nodded: I know, I took caffeine today and it made me crazy — Actually it made me think of you, I said (because, really, it had).

And he went on —

It's like anything, though, I mean like any drug — Once you're on it you can't just stop, I'm taking five pills a day, I can't stop right now — But I can't fucking take this —

Okay, I said, It's only one more week, yeah? We're almost done and then it ends and you can stop — Or — Wait, Are you going to Quebec?

(Quebec was the next planting contract that year, like New Brunswick had been previously, for the ones who wanted to continue working through August.)

He paused a moment.

I applied for another job, he said — With the Company, and if I get that job, then I don't have to plant — But otherwise I'm going to Quebec, yeah.

So I stopped and looked at him and said, I really hope you get that job,

And he said, Yeah.

We were sitting compactly under the raining greyness, facing each other, and the words had slowed down, somewhat. Less urgency, somewhat. Konrad rolled up on the quad — the second quad, not the one that was upside down in a ditch.

Ben stood, and walked to Konrad and said blankly:

I can't plant another fucking tree.

But slower now, and resignedly.

Konrad looked at him, without a smile on, and said this:

I'll drive you back to your land.

And that wasn't a bargain, or a question, or an order; it was just solidarity, now, because they both knew, as I knew, that Ben was going to plant trees for the rest of the day,

And for the rest of the week, and for another month at least.

And that's how it went. When the contract was over, he went to Quebec, and he planted more trees.

No one exchanged any more words, then. Ben stepped onto the quad, stood beside Konrad and leaned back with one hand hooked into the steel rack, and the quad ripped the silence apart and off they went.

I went back to my own land, then, and the caffeine went fizzling out and I finished the day mechanically like always, because sometimes it isn't really worth it to do anything more than that.

79

We were home late, very late. And wet and tired and fizzling out, and we all shoved ourselves inside of the mess tent for dinner. We sat down to shove spaghetti into our mouths, full urgency, and that was when we heard there was a bear in camp.

It was just one of those rumours that floats around — Yeah, a bear's been hanging out and bugging the cooks all day — Eh, that's pretty annoying I guess —

I was sitting with Korry and Travis and I was spewing words at them. I was supposed to be getting a bone scan the next day, and now I was feeling bad about missing a day of work — They're not going to tell me anything, I said, And the contract's almost over, Why even bother, and Should I cancel it,

And we aren't even allowed to go to the hospital, I said,

And someone answered: That isn't what he said — I don't think Tom was talking about you, when he said that,

And someone answered: Well, why don't you cancel it then,

And I ranted something like,

So now Tom has to drive me to the hospital and he's gonna be a fucking asshole about it —

Which in reality was not the issue. If I had an issue with Tom at all, it was more to the effect that, in reality, I had a great deal of respect for him.

And now I'm missing a day of work, I said.

I always felt sick by then, couldn't finish my food and pushed my dish across to Travis. And I kept going in the same voice that Ben had been using that afternoon —

It's stupid to have a hospital thing tomorrow, This is fucking ridiculous —

And that's when Korry looked at me and said:

Look, man, You gotta get over it.

I thought about that and thought, Yeah, okay, that's a good point.

I was still trying to get over it.

80

They named the bear Reggie. I don't know who named it or why, I just heard that that was its name.

Tom leaned on a truck horn to call a meeting about the bear after dinner. At that point I was standing by the water barrels with Stefan. We were brushing our teeth and discussing the most obvious highlight of the day:

Stefan said maybe breakfast but probably dinner and I said, Tooth-brushing, Because it's like a miniature massage and Plus you get to go to sleep afterwards —

And he said, Also it's the only part of your body that will ever feel clean —

And then Tom was leaning on the horn and we wondered what that was all about.

Sixty of us converged in a haphazard circle by the vans, shuffling about and chattering, and as we did Reggie came peeking out of the treeline by the shitters. Maybe two hundred metres away from the crowd, then — this lanky black bear clambered out onto edge of the gravel plain. He stopped and looked at us, and we all looked at him,

And Tom turned to us all, slowly smiling, said:

So you might have heard, There's a bear in camp.

And he told us there wasn't much we could do about it tonight. It was already past 9 pm by then and we didn't have too many options — I mean, we didn't have a gun or anything —

So everyone take your tents away from the treeline, because the bear is going to stick to the treeline mostly — And it's best if everyone consolidates tents tonight, stay close together and the bear won't come near —

And he said, It really wouldn't be a bad idea to bring your shovel to bed with you —

Him smiling but also completely serious.

Meanwhile Reggie himself came lumbering out along the slope, nosing his way towards a little clump of tents perched right up against the charred black-green forest. And then suddenly Krystal was yelling, full-volume, from the edge of the crowd where we were all gathered, yelling —

Don't you fucking DARE go near my tent —

And then she yelled, FUCK I just put a fucking bag of GARBAGE in there!

And people starting to laugh and stir and someone said, Why the fuck did you do that?

Then Krystal broke away from the group and went charging towards the bear and screaming at it,

GET THE FUCK AWAY FROM MY TENT

Reggie was still about two hundred metres away from us and strolling sedately into the group of tents, following the scent of garbage I suppose,

So in the interest of Krystal remaining un-mauled, everyone started to follow her, walking together in this massive laughing clump, like a really slow-motion cavalry, and Stefan beside me was quietly half-smiling commentating,

This is like a lynch mob, he said.

We all advanced on poor Reggie, and he stopped and looked up at us again, and he hesitated. Some rookie had an air horn and was blowing it as a kind of warning signal, and Reggie started to back up.

Tom took the air horn and walked out in front of us, followed Reggie as he fled, and Tom walked alone, directly up to the edge of the treeline just blasting this horn. Meanwhile from inside of the crowd, Miko, the camp dog, came bounding suddenly and charged full speed into the bushes after the bear. We just heard some rustling, and —

I kind of held my breath and hoped that the dog was going to come back out, and not bleeding —

Sure enough, Miko came out prancing, tail high. Like the proudest, happiest animal you've ever seen. Almost dancing with the thrill of his own dominance, he dove into a puddle on the gravel there and went rolling around and splashing, and pretty much laughing with the rest of us.

The group started to disperse after a while. I went with Hannah and Megan back to our triad of tents. Mine was just inside the treeline so the three of us picked it up, awkwardly, with all the clothes and bedding making a sagging weight in the centre, and we (laughing) lifted and carried it down onto the flat plain.

The main issue wasn't really safety, for me. It was more about that thing that happens when you wake up at two or three in the morning, blind in the dark, and you remember half-sleeping that there's some kind of a scavenging black shadow out there, and then you start listening to the rustling in the bushes around you and your sleep is off all night, then, and that just isn't worth it.

So we brought mine out into the open, and then our tents were all so close together we'd be able to have an easy conversation from inside our sleeping bags. It was like some kind of preteen slumber party, and we giggled at that — How exciting —

Hm, I asked Hannah — Do you think we should bring our shovels to bed?

And she said:

I was thinking about that too, but my shovel's really far away right now and I don't want to walk over there.

And I looked over towards the vans, towards where our shovels and planting bags were all scattered about across the ground, and it was maybe one hundred metres away, and I said, Yeah definitely too far.

I picked up a rock, some jagged skull-sized hunk of stone, and I told Hannah,

Okay this will be my bear-clubbing rock, I'm definitely going to club a bear to death with this bear-clubbing rock tonight.

And she said:

You should label it, you know, So you don't get confused and use the wrong rock by accident,

And I brought this rock to the front door of my tent before bed and considered the problem solved.

The problem was more decisively solved with a twelve-gauge shotgun a few minutes later.

I'd crawled back out of my tent because in all of the excitement I'd forgotten to fill my water canteen for the night, and that was too important to ignore.

I was walking towards the mess tent when I ran into Arron and we started hanging around and chatting, and then I glanced over and saw Reggie come strolling out of the treeline in the exact spot where my tent had been a few minutes earlier. We watched him from some distance: nose poking along in front of him, shaggy tree-trunk legs, and oversized ears that were somehow mouselike. We watched him sniffing his way out of the bush, a couple of metres from where Hannah and Megan were lying in bed.

The bear wandered away behind the cookshack, and started nosing around in the slurry pit there, and then slowly he went wading right into it.

That's just gross, man, I said and I laughed.

Arron and I walked along parallel to the bear, following from a distance just to enjoy the show. Tom had just driven into camp again, and he got out of the truck and joined us and said —

Don't do anything to scare it off eh,

And the three of us just stood, strolled, observed.

Reggie was happily sloshing about in the slurry pit, when a foreign red pickup truck came rolling in. Out came a grizzled silver-haired man in denim and flannel, carrying a twelve-gauge shotgun. He was the owner of the Campground across the road.

There was just a clump of us still awake and we crowded into the mouth of the mess tent, out of the way but still watching the main event. It was turning grey outside, and Reggie was just a shadow now, but we saw his head perk up. He looked around and suddenly skittish he backed away, backed into the belt of forest again, and he disappeared into just an extra-black blackness between the trees. The bushes were vaguely rustling, the twilight was deepening,

And the shotgun went off, explosively.

We heard more rustling after the shot was fired. Louder rustling, clumsier. They waited a few minutes and then Tom and Ceilidh took flashlights and walked into the bushes, to see.

We heard they found blood but no body.

The Campground Owner told us that Reggie was in the lake by now — that they always go to the water to die.

81

Bennett was in the hospital, still. He didn't get the bloodwork back about MRSA until after we'd all left Timmins, so still no one knew what these infections actually were — not in technical terms anyway.

But of course we knew by then that they were contagious. We knew that Bennett was waiting on an operation and that the whole thing had become fairly serious.

Andreas's infection was monstrous. Andreas was a long-haired highballer who planted the same way Arron did, with the same kind of wiry athleticism, strategy and cool endless energy.

(Different from Ben, who seemed to burn ferociously through the days.)

After the incident with Bennett, Tom told Andreas that he needed to have his infection checked out again. Andreas had already seen a doctor and was already taking antibiotics, but then, Bennett had been too. Tom took Andreas to the hospital late at night on that Day Off, to see if there was chance that this was going to spread to the bloodstream.

But Andreas didn't have a fever, and the medical professional told him that his infection was less risky than Bennett's had been, since it was mid-thigh as opposed to on the knee, and it wouldn't so easily spread to the bone. So they sent him home — or rather, back to camp — and Andreas continued working through it.

I saw his infection on the morning of Day 64, before I went into town for my bone scan. It had rained again, at night, and the mess tent was flooded at either end but not as badly as it had been before. We were gathering for the morning meeting out front, in the damp greyness of mist and puddling gravel. Andreas pulled his pants down at someone's request and we looked and grimaced at the sight of it.

His whole leg was bright red, with the skin stretched tight. I could see some fluid like pus running in swollen vertical streams over his muscle.

I said to him, That looks painful —
Which was somewhat of an understatement —
And he grinned at me and said,
It hurts like a bitch when I'm planting.

82

I spent the rest of that morning drifting through stages of medical procedure in a state of limp passivity. I sat in a chair for maybe fifteen minutes to wait on the injection and was asleep immediately. In an almost dreamlike state I had something injected into my arm and I asked the nurse what it was, and she said,

This is a radioactive substance from Chalk River.

I smiled about the ominous-sounding vagueness of that statement and I said,

Great.

The radioactive substance was supposed to be attracted to areas of calcium turnover, and would show up in the scan, thus demonstrating locations of significant healing activity — injury or infection — in the bone.

So I waited for a couple of hours while the injection went creeping around in my body. I waited in the emergency waiting room, which felt like home by then, and that was where I ran into Jess — Bennett's girlfriend.

It was surprising at first. It was one of those moments when you chance to meet someone who seems vaguely familiar and you aren't certain where from. She was wearing real clothes, jeans and t-shirt and sneakers, and her blonde hair was loose and clean and straight, and there wasn't any dirt on her face — so that was all quite startling to me. And I was surprised and happy to see her, and it felt like it had been a long long time.

She was stuck in town, staying in the hotel, waiting on Bennett's operation and driving B's personal vehicle around. After Bennett was hooked up to IV, the professional determined that the infection wasn't in his blood yet, but would need to be scraped out of his knee, surgically, in order to prevent it from reaching the bone. His operation was low-priority and was repeatedly being rescheduled, so Jess had been waiting two days, now, since the accident. She was keeping him company and waiting to drive him back to camp as soon as the operation had actually taken place. This was stressful, she said,

Because I feel like I should be planting right now, and I'm just stuck here doing nothing — But Tom said they can't spare anyone in Management to wait on him so the best thing I can do is stick around town — It's kind of driving me crazy,

And when I asked about Bennett, well:

He feels really bad that Parks and Yukon have to work double to cover for him now, and he's super bored and wants to go back to work — He's mostly pissed off about flipping the truck because he can't be on the block right now.

Yeah, yeah of course —

I told her about the excitement in camp, everything she'd missed, which was mostly just Reggie the bear.

She hadn't heard anything of it. The only person Jess had been in contact with was Tom — and only to send him updates on Bennett and the surgery. The two previous nights, she said, the operation kept getting pushed back, over and over. It was scheduled for midnight, 2 am, 4 am, and so on —

I've been texting Tom, she said, Literally all night for the past two nights and he's always responded — I mean, he's responded to me at three, four, five in the morning, right away — I actually don't think he's slept at all.

Jess spoke clear and steady, her eyebrows just slightly furrowed. She told me: Actually I don't know when he last slept — Actually I think Tom's doing twenty-four-hour days right now, which is insane.

I agreed that it was insane. I told her that there was talk in camp, now, that the eight-day shift wasn't going to kill it — that it wouldn't be enough to finish the contract. There were too many trees still to be planted, and there were too many things going wrong: there were still frozen seedlings along with a missing deliverer, and there were all of the planter injuries and absences. There were rookies who were throwing in the towel, now, or going home for personal reasons. Someone had a sick grandmother and someone had a sick girlfriend to go back to, and then there were some who were just dropping off. Simply it had gone on too long, and people had other places to be.

Jess and I looked at each other. There was that sense of urgency; there was the fact that you can't just stop. Our people were on the block and we should have been there with them. It wasn't like we really wanted to be planting trees — But certainly, certainly we didn't want to *not* be planting trees.

83

The nurse showed me the results of the bone scan as soon as it was finished. I looked at an image of my own skeleton, conjured up in grainy white against a black screen. The radioactive Chalk River substance showed up in clusters of electric blue like pointilism, sparsely dotted throughout. In the base of my left leg, the electric blue consolidated sharply: the bottom half of the shin was completely alight with it.

Yes, there's definitely something going on there, said the nurse; It definitely could be an infection, Yes; You definitely have to come back for the other two appointments.

Which didn't tell me anything new, and nothing specific: the scan confirmed that there was healing activity — that there was something, yes — but what? The only thing I gained from it was the affirmation that at least I wasn't making it up. At least I was sane — in some way or another. At least there was that.

I went back to the waiting room, where Tom said he'd meet me to take me to back to work. It was approaching noon by then.

Tom had gone in to check on Bennett, who was doing alright but was infinitely bored and restless. When he came back into the waiting room, Tom sat down with me and said we were waiting on Yukon to arrive now. There was a new plan in place: Yukon would take me into the block, and I would work as a deliverer again, so that we could try to match the Push-to-Finish pace while short-handed. In the end Yukon and I worked all afternoon and up until sunset. We rotated some hundred-thousand frozen trees out of the latest reefer, onto the ground to thaw, and we set up a block for the next day. Because no matter what, no matter how many things were going wrong, the trees and the land needed to be ready and the planters needed to be planting — Full urgency.

Tom and I waited, briefly, for Yukon. Tom sat low in one of the vinyl-steel chairs, and he leaned his head against the wall and looked wildly out of place in the scrubbed-white hospital setting. Too much tan and dust and scruff, too much hardness and outdoors.

Tom asked how the bone scan had gone. Absently, looking halfway up towards the white-tile ceiling.

I told him:

My leg lit up, on the scan, so it means there's something going on — Might be a bone infection, might be a healing fracture.

He glanced at me slow and half-smiled: Isn't that exactly what you already knew?

And I glanced away, half-smiled,

Yeah, Exactly.

Paused for a moment and said:

Look, I don't know if these tests are going to tell me anything, And if the contract is going to be over so soon, Then maybe I should just plant to the end of it, and get this thing dealt with afterwards, instead.

And Tom — actually looked at me, then: eyes deep blue and bloodshot.

That's fucking stupid, he said.

I half-laughed.

You'll go to all the appointments, he said slowly, And you'll be happy about it.

And I said, Okay.

I half-laughed, Okay.

And I almost wanted to say Thank You but I didn't.

And then I was allowed to stop thinking about it again.

84

Day 65: some day in a swamp with the air made out of mosquitoes.

Since I was at the hospital the day before, I'd lent my bugspray to Rodrigo, and now I missed it.

It occurred to me that maybe I was annoyed at Rodrigo for still having my bugspray that day,

And then it occurred to me that really I wasn't. There were things biting me and really I didn't care.

Which was interesting.

I mean really I didn't care, and certainly I couldn't be bothered to get annoyed.

Out of habit I blew my breath out in streams to keep the insects off of my lips, and I moved around at some dull-moderate pace, and I guess ten hours went by.

85

The final week of the contract or so, the cooks started taking suggestions from the planters and making everything, so that later on we had sushi and poutine together at the same meal, and whatever else it was that anyone was asking for.

(Lovely, Ceilidh, Thank you)

Day 65 I was sitting around a table with the girls and we were shovelling food into ourselves despite that ever-present nausea — same as how we lay horizontal at night, and closed our eyes despite the insomnia.

Hannah had laryngitis then and she spoke like she was half-dead. She was barely rasping these words out, sounding like a robot with low batteries, and I told her,

Stop it Hannah, You sound like you are dying.

Do you want me to stop speaking? she said,

And I said, I don't know, I just meant Stop sounding like you're dying I guess,

Because it was painful to hear her speak.

Megan, at dinner that night, told us she'd thrown up in her land. She said she hadn't even seen it coming, hadn't even felt nauseous but then suddenly she'd been vomiting against the black muck, and she said, Well I was working pretty hard, So I guess that's why —

It was a hot day, Yeah —

And she said she'd been working so hard that her crew boss, B, had given her the greatest compliment she'd ever received from him, which was this:

You are more than adequate.

But he'd also said, the same day,

I hate your face,

So perhaps it evened out.

And we were laughing, then, about that.

Krystal was telling us that she kept seeing these new bugs in her land, and they were shaped like this:

(she drew a squiggle in the air to illustrate it)

And these bugs flew, and they moved faster than mosquitoes but they were the size of deerflies —

And we all started to laugh, because, Sorry, What, though?

And Hannah at some point asked what it meant if she was peeing brown —

Yeah, like, really — Brown —

And we decided it meant Too Much Caffeine.

(She nodded, True, I've been leaning on the caffeine lately)

Yes, Brown pee means Dehydration, Yeah, That would do it,

And Megan said B had told her she could stop early, that afternoon, because he saw her hit a hornets' nest —

He saw her stick the shovel in, then drop the shovel and run, getting stung three times, and there was only a half-hour left in the day, so B (laughed and then) said she could stop if she wanted, and he would understand.

And did you stop? I said,

And she said, No, I mean, What else was I going to do — Sit on the side of the road?

So she'd sprinted in to retrieve her shovel and then planted another bag after that.

Korry was walking past us, on the way to the dishes sink, as the shadows were lengthening and the four of us — Megan Hannah Krystal and I — were slumping around our white-plastic table and laughing about god-knows-what,

And Megan called to Korry — Eh, hey,

Hey have you seen any bugs in your land that are shaped like seahorses and move faster than mosquitoes?

And Korry said, Man, Those are hummingbirds,

And I just put my forehead onto the table and laughed, and had tears in my eyes, and laughed and couldn't stop,

While darkness came down around us to signal another day done.

86

Day 66, I hit a hornets' nest myself, early on. I was stung three times on the outside of my left leg, and then I thought of Megan — the same story, the day before — so I didn't drop my shovel and instead I just ran. I skipped across a pile of slash and started smiling to myself.

Smooth stinging pains blossoming along the side of my leg, on top of the rest of it. I planted a tree, and as I leaned over, I made my breath go louder so that it was a sigh, a cathartic SIGH,

And then I kept planting trees, but faster.

Halfway through the day we were all moved somewhere new, together. It was Arron, Jake, Travis, and I. We all finished our land together, sprinting about in these swampy furrows and making a real time of it.

I was still, still, listening to the same twelve songs on repeat — approaching three hundred times in a row, now.

And Konrad took us up together and dumped us somewhere new:

I don't know much about it, but Yukon said maybe it was an ecological experiment, because instead of a regular clear-cut this was a field, and it was full of still-standing broad-canopied deciduous trees, which was a strange sight for us. Then in between the leafy arbols, there was thick green tangled growth that was taller than we were —

Which was, evidently, not a strange sight for us at all.

Konrad was being nice and being fair, and he sent the whole crew in side-by-side so we could finish that little section of land all together — rather than leaving just one or two planters drowning suicidal in that murky green sea.

And then, somehow, it all started to get funny. We couldn't see each other; we were all invisible to each other and we were all completely lost because these bushes were taller than we were, and we were fighting them with every step. But we could hear each other moving, not so far away, kind of close together,

So then we found ourselves all standing, standing on high, climbing up onto boulders, onto stumps and logs, and then we could just-barely see each other over the swaying field.

On my left was Jake's orange hard hat, and on my right, Travis's.

In front of us, Ben and Brad were planting together and we were all trying to work out who was supposed to be where, but we couldn't even see our own flagger. Then Arron was just past Jake, and Rodrigo beyond him —

One of the boys was yelling out at me,

You wanna have an in-lander?

And I didn't hear — I yelled back, What?

You wanna have an in-lander?

Which is, hey, a bold sexual proposition, and I yelled laughing —

Fucking *way* too many thorns!

We ducked back inside of them, all trapped inside these green cages, and each of us just thrashing —

And a few minutes later found ourselves climbing up, again, above the leafy-green ceiling, and I yelled at them,

Fuck, this is hilarious!

Jake replied, What part of this is funny — ?

I laughed to him — ALL of it!

And I believed it, too.

I ducked back underneath, and I heard him laughing, then, too.

§ § § §

That day as I blindly strode forward — full speed! — I slammed my shin into a stump. The left shin, midway up.

I almost collapsed and cried. I felt the tears there, behind my eyes, but then I just kept planting trees.

I rolled forward, and forward, and I kept my vision down towards the green-shrouded ground, and eventually I found the perfect little thing:

This slice of log, the rotting outer-shell of bark from some dying tree, soft and thick and spongey.

I picked it up, stuck it into the back of my planting bags, and when I reached the roadside I duct-taped this bark-barrel over my leg — the same as Konrad and I had done with the bus manual, a month prior.

And — Wow, what a development —

It was the perfect shin pad.

I no longer had to worry about smashing my shin into a stump or a log or a branch. I just kept running —

And there was a piece of bark taped over my leg,

And it felt amazing — No, really, it felt amazing.

87

Konrad met me on the roadside that day and asked me how it was going, and I told him:

Fucking amazing, I'm about to PB,

And he smiled and informed me pleasantly,

You're bleeding from your neck —

To which I grinned and said,

Great, I can't feel pain.

Good, he said, still smiling, and me smiling, too,

So I charged back in, and actually I did hit a PB that day — and also the following day,

And another two days after that.

88

That's how it happened. My production almost doubled, very suddenly.

Something snapped into place. Suddenly everything was motion, and all the obstacles disappeared. It was an incredible place to be.

Parts of this were gradual, of course: the technical improvements, the muscle memory. By that time I'd been doing this thing for three seasons, more or less. I'd been practicing the same movements every day all day, for more than six full months of my life.

So I don't remember at what point, exactly, the tree planting itself became easy. I can't remember any specific day when the land finally made sense — when I finally earned the x-ray vision to see through the layers on the ground, to read through the duff-moss-logs-rocks, and to simply know — and to automatically put the tip of a shovel right inside of a tiny, invisible pocket of soil, every time.

And I don't know when, exactly, I no longer had any use for flagger — when I could simply remember where I'd been, where I'd walked, where I'd planted and where I hadn't — when I could recognize one rock from the next, and tell the difference between each and every fallen birch, each and every sawed-off stump. There simply came a time when I understood the land — any land — well enough to know, and never have to stop or think.

And there came a time, too, when my feet ceased to ache under the weight of the trees, and when my skin became leather and ceased to bleed and the insect bites ceased to itch and the muscles in my arms and back and legs ceased to burn.

Gradual changes, months in the making. These were the results of practice: nothing else, and these were the markings of any solid veteran. These things arrived, eventually, and everything ceased to be overwhelming.

At what point? Gradually.

But there was something else, for me, too. Something which was sudden. And I can mark, clearly enough, the point where this changed and suddenly, yes, my numbers doubled —

And more than just the numbers. Most things changed, somehow, all of a sudden, after that.

In the final week of the contract, it wasn't just about practice or patience or the gradual effects of time —

It was an electric jolt into high awareness, total clarity, full commitment.

How, why?

You just reach a certain point.

Really, things had started getting too real. There was pressure, exhaustion, excitement, pain — and I didn't know, anymore, if it was going to be okay. My thoughts were running in circles for a while and then they just went numb. And I felt sick and hurt, and as far as I could tell I didn't have anything left to give, and I really didn't care either way.

Fuckless, fuckless and fucking exhausted — and I kept going anyway.

And what happened, then, was that I let go of everything.

I let go of *everything* —

And that might have been the most difficult and most rewarding thing I'd ever done.

That was when I stumbled into focus, and everything came into focus for me. That was when I found that it was possible to focus on this thing — on this dreadful mundane task — this urgent ugly chore —

To focus on *tree planting* —

With such a degree of hyperattention that everything else disappeared. The only thing left was motion.

Motion,

And with it — inexplicably, unexpectedly — this rapt sense of euphoria.

And with that — ineffable and unbidden — a wild and half-crazed, life-changing and beautiful revelation.

It's true. That happened.

That made everything worth it. I think that changed my life.

Day 66, I was stung by three bees and I smiled about it, and I planted faster and it felt good. Day 66 I duct-taped a piece of rotting log over my shin and every part of my being lit up with gratitude, suddenly, because I could walk a little more freely. I could move faster without hitting that godforsaken soft spot, and I was smiling about it for hours, and then I was laughing about it, too. And I had no complaints about anything, and nothing — nothing — was bad.

Day 67, I realized that nothing had ever been bad, and everything was only good. Thirty-seven degrees Celsius that day, and I was running up and down hills of sunbaked sand. There was dust in my throat and sweat in my eyes, and I thought that the powerlines hanging over the back of my clearcut were the most beautiful things I'd ever seen. The sky was blue and I was surrounded by shredded logs and upturned earth and deerfies, and I was climbing all over everything with full speed and full urgency — because I knew suddenly that everything was temporary anyway — because I was hit, almost physically, by the understanding that everything, and anything, and everything, was impermanent and imperfect — and suddenly that made sense. Suddenly I was in love with the sun and the dirt and the deerflies, and the only thing I could do to celebrate it all was to move — move faster — and there had never been anything more important than that.

Day 69, thirty-eight degrees Celsius and I was darting in spirals across a rainbow-coloured sphagnum swamp and I was bleeding profusely out of my nose. At some point Yukon yelled at me, out the window of his truck: I am so proud of you, so fucking proud of you — and his face was gleaming and then he rocketed off — onward to glory. 4 pm, the thunderstorm struck and everything turned to water and lightning again, and Konrad pulled us out to hide in the van. So maybe an hour was ripped out of the day and still I moved faster and harder than I ever had before. Everything was water, deep spongy water after that: hard rain, soft moss and liquid slick swamp, and I fell hips-deep into a moat of opaque muck. Travis saw me fall and he cupped his hands around his mouth and yelled at me, from afar — You are a beautiful goddess, You are an Amazonian warrior! — so I was laughing, too, and I planted a tree in the bank of the swamp before climbing out, dripping filth-black, and I climbed out running, running faster —

Faster, because time was running out.

Those days I thought about other places that I could be — other places that I would rather be — and there were none. There was nothing else. I was sweating and bleeding under a blinding bare sun, or I was soaked deep in thunderclouds, and I thought about real life —

Real Life, as we called it. I thought of the city, of humans seated behind the windows of skyscraping buildings — I thought of comfort and leisure and traffic and phone calls — I thought of money — of people wearing clothes and wearing faces —

And I knew that I wasn't missing out on any of it. Just for an instant, I knew that none of that was as real as what I had, right there and then, already. I had it all, already; I had everything. I had air in my lungs and my people around me —

And I had nothing to worry about and nothing to fear.

Here, look — This is what's really important:

I also had this weak leg. One weak leg, remember? I could feel it all the time, and it hurt, and it kept telling me:

Do you remember? — that's what my leg was saying — Do you remember being twenty years old and almost ceasing to be alive, on some unspectacular morning in October beneath a stack of falling wood? Do you remember what it feels like to be crushed against a slab of polished concrete below the weight of some thoughtless unstoppable thing? The weight of this thing, and the sensation of it — stronger than your bones and your heart —

Remember these unstoppable things that will stop your blood from pumping and your thoughts from flowing. Remember that your thoughts and your feelings, your words and your sensations, and everything you have ever been —

That all of these things will stop, and irreversibly undeniably they will stop — on some unremarkable day in October, or in any standard month of any routine year of what was once your life — and unexpectedly, accidentally —

Do you remember that you are temporary, too?

Yes, I remembered it then, and that was when everything made sense.

I had one weak leg, and I was still running. And I had three good limbs and a damn strong back, and I had this reminder that everything was just a fleeting instant, and that every beautiful and every terrible thing was only out on a loan.

That was it, then. That was the only thing I'd ever felt certain of —

That everything ends, and everything will end, but it was a good thing that it happened, anyway.

Then I let go. I let go, and I found focus — hard focus —
And, suddenly, peace:
Peace, in the sand and the swamp and the birdsong — in the shadows, and the deep green treeline hovering in lines all around — in the damp sweet scent of rotting logs, of rainbowy mosses — in the overbright sunlight, knifelike and burning — the taste of sweat, the taste of blood — heavy clothes hanging wetly, and heady thick thunder overhead — soaking feet and fingertips, rolling bentbacked strides — forward, always forward — and deep, deep-as-the-ocean fatigue —
And all of that was beautiful, I swear. All of it was only good.

89

The moment passed. Moments tend to.
I guess you can't spend a whole lifetime running around inside of a euphoric inferno. Eventually you just have to go to sleep. And eventually, probably, you have to re-engage with normalcy, with the day-to-day, in some form or another.

Eventually I crashed, physically. I thought it was a bone infection on the very last night in camp, Day 71. I wound up shaking and burning in a fetal curl on top of my sleeping bag, that night while the guys were whipping each other with belts under the rain-pummeled tarp of the mess tent. I thought I was really truly sick, then, because my vision was going black of its own accord — but I guess what actually happened is that I just burned out.
It catches up to you, that's all. The point is, I didn't have a bone infection.

90

As Jess and I had predicted in the hospital waiting room, the eight-day shift didn't kill it. In the middle of the week, Day 68, we had to take a Day Off, so that the unfreezing trees could catch up and the planters could try to recover.

That final Night Off in camp, Bennett was released from the hospital. He'd spent four days waiting on surgery, and on Day 66 he'd finally had the operation. It was straightforward and successful. They cleaned out his knee, scraped the infection from the bone, and bandaged it up. He'd been bent on returning to work after that. He said he felt fine; he was ready to re-engage in the Push-to-Finish.

The medical professionals nixed it: No, Not a chance. There was a gaping hole on the side of Bennett's knee, now, deep like a bullet wound, since all the fluid had been scraped out. He wanted to go back to work — back to living in the same tent, the same sleeping bag — back to the sweat and the block-filth and all the same old —

Not a chance, they said. Bennett was forced off the contract. He came back on Day 67 and said goodbye to his brothers-in-arms: Tom, Yukon, Parks, and the crew bosses. Then the real world took him back.

Jess, of course, came back to work until the contract was done — the very last shift, just three final days.

91

Day 69, in that waterlogged swamp beneath the rolling thunderstorm, I hit my own important Personal Best. On the following day, Day 70, all thirteen of my crew members hit theirs. That was our final full day of tree planting, and it couldn't really have gone any better.

Personally, I missed half of the day because I was receiving a gallium injection at the hospital. The gallium was injected into my blood and left to circulate for two days in preparation for the final scan, which would be the bone infection test.

Tom picked me up from the hospital after the appointment and he drove me into the block. We met Parks' truck on the way in, and they pulled up to each other, driver-side to driver-side, to talk business.

Then Parks leaned out of his window and told me:

You're about to go into the best land you've ever seen.

And I said, Great.

Parks looked at me, paused, replied:

I can't tell if you're excited about that or angry.

And I thought about it — Was I angry to have missed half the day in the best land I'd ever seen, or excited to still have half the day in front of me?

I smiled at him and spoke honestly:

I'm completely apathetic, I said.

Tom smiled too, and corrected me —

Completely *pa*thetic.

And I grinned.

92

Parks was right about the land; it wasn't just the old Management cliche. It was the best land I'd ever seen: the oft-alleged, oft-dreamed-of, straight sandy furrows — saved for the final full day. It was everyone's last chance at glory.

And everyone did it. See:

81,000 trees between thirteen-and-a-half planters is an average of 6,000 each. Some more, some less,

All of them PBs.

Well, maybe not mine. Not technically — But for a half-day, it was pretty damn good.

Golden light and the long shadows of evening:

Our crew was giddily planting the last few seedlings into soft sandy roadsides. Our van was parked on a landing overseeing the wide plateaus of parallel furrows, and we gravitated towards it, ambling along in groups of three or four.

There was laughter there, hugs, and wide wide smiles there. There was Parks walking between the planters shaking their hands and grinning,

Good Wrap, he said — like sports teams saying Good Game — facetious, sure, and yet genuine, glowing —

Good Wrap.

Three of our people — Jake, Arron, Ben — planted more than 7,000 trees each that day. That's barely human; that's almost impossible. That's a rare kind of athleticism — and focus — some deep hard focus.

So when everyone collected around each other, what was there but that drunken high of full-body exhaustion, of dust and sweat and laughter: tangible and contagious. We could taste it in the air, we could swim in it, suddenly weightless. For a brief moment, there was that high sensation that nothing is bad, that nothing has ever been bad.

In the van we drove home all stuck together again at the shoulders and legs. That's when we found out that Hannah's day had gone sour. She didn't want anyone to know. She was smiling. Apologetically, she was smiling — I'm so sorry that this happened to me, Please don't worry, I really don't mind at all —

She'd been working by a logging road that had cottage-country traffic on it. There were real people moving back and forth, a truck or two passing sporadically, over the length of the eleven-hour day.

And while Hannah was bentbacked out in the land, some real person stopped by her cache and rifled through her backpack, stole her camera.

The following day every one of her crew members donated the earnings from one of the bundles they planted. Hannah was forced to claim an extra hundred-fifty-so dollars, earned by her crew on the final day of work, to compensate for her unlucky loss.

It was something like this:

There was no one looking out for us, out there, unless we were looking out for each other. So that's what we did.

93

The very final workday was the 71st day of the contract. It was short, and smooth, and raining. We finished early, all together, and then everything was done and everything was over, more or less.

I stopped planting perhaps earlier than anyone. I put a few hundred trees in, moving side-by-side with Arron, and then the land was starting to wrap up. I padded out onto the deep rain-dappled sand of the roadside and I ran into Konrad and said, Hey,

Can I stop planting now?

And I thought he might have been joking when he said, Yep.

I looked him dead in the face: No, Are you serious? Can I stop planting now?

That eternal, indecipherable Konrad-smile. He shrugged:

If you want to.

For sure? Actual?

Sure.

Like forever?

The same smile, a little bit deeper:

You're done.

So I jumped on him. I wrapped my arms and legs around him and he took a half-step back and then hugged me too. And I clung onto him and shouted over his shoulder —

I'm never planting another tree in my life.

I'm never planting another tree ever! Ever in my life!

I disengaged, grinning hard, and I dropped to my knees in the sand and buried my hands in it. Felt the dampish sand between my fingers, the rain hissing soft into my shoulders, and I watched Konrad-smiling still working away.

The roles all got shuffled, that day. Konrad wound up delivering. Yukon was planting trees. Travis took the role of crew boss and moved around making a parody of it. Our young-girl-Client-quality-checkers were carrying trees for the highballers, who just kept pounding them in — still racing to the finish line.

Ben planted his two-hundred-thousandth tree of the season, that day. That's how many trees it took to highball the camp.

I didn't plant at all, after the first couple of hours in the morning. I didn't do anything; all the roles had been filled. I climbed on top of the van and stood there in the rain. Everything was grey howling-wind and wet, and I watched all of the planters moving along together — all the ones who were still going straight to the end. Thirty people, maybe, back and forth in lines, side-by-side. I watched them from above and they turned into insects again: fluorescent-coloured hard-shelled beetles crawling about in clumps through the debris.

The metal roof of the van was cold and rain-beaded and slippery-wet. I couldn't stop smiling. I was smiling for so long that it would have hurt my face, if I hadn't been immune to pain.

Mid-morning we were finished. All of the trees gone. It was something like six million trees. Someone, somewhere, has a

more accurate number. It's written in the paperwork, somewhere — but I don't know very much about the paperwork.

It was something like six million trees — and I don't know
the exact number but I know exactly what it took. One tree
at a time, six million times. One endless day at a time, two
aching steps at a time. Indefinite and infuriating and a little
bit incredible, in a way.

Something like six million trees, left to grow — more or
less —

Maybe another eighty years, if they're lucky. Eighty years
and they're ready to be cut down. Even then, they'll be around
longer than we will.

94

Maybe noon, we were consolidating up on a hillside. Wet
burnt-up greenness and creamy sand under thickly brood-
ing clouds. It was still morning and we were throwing off
our hard hats and someone was dunking their head in the
black swamp moat — and then someone else was shoved into
it — and someone was rolling around in it. Blackened and
dripping with muck, didn't matter anymore. Hadn't mattered for a long time, now.

We clumped on the hillside and faced the road. Fifty or
so people — everyone who made it through to the last day.
Stood together, arms across shoulders, standing in rows up
the hill so everyone's faces would be showing.

One of our planters set up a tripod on the plateau below,
in front of the swampwater where they'd been frolicking a
minute prior. We stood and faced the camera, waited for the
shutter-click.

Fifty people, isolated together on a burnt-up hillside next
to a logging road. No one else around, just trees and birds,

maybe snakes and spiders and bears, and clouds and rain but no humans except for us.

And we were all just standing there, in a silent clump, looking at this three-legged cyclops and waiting —

And then everyone started to laugh.

The cyclops sat and looked at us, black and spindly and still.

Why is it staring at me! shouted Gabe.

It's fucking creepy! someone was hollering,

And, What the fuck is going on right now!

Everyone shouting and laughing, everything consumed again by absurdity — always absurdity — and the camera shutter clicked.

I saw the photo a few months later; the Company sent it to each of us on a postcard. Fifty-some smiles, absurd grins blindingly white against soot-blackened faces. Fifty-some human beings all tethered like a raft in this sea of green bush, mud-blackened and haggard in the rain, and fifty identical grins.

95

I didn't say goodbye to anyone except for Yukon. We kept saying goodbye over and over again: four times, because we didn't know when it would actually be the last time. He went west, I went south. What else do you say? Just a hug and an easy See Ya Later. Not very sentimental.

He was the only one I said goodbye to; everyone else I walked away from, when Yukon and I took the garbage to the dump in the middle of camp teardown on Day 72. It was more than one tonne of garbage: I know because we weighed the trailer on the way into the landfill site. Yukon and I carried out all the bags and the unwanted shit, a thousand handfuls of unwanted shit, and we threw it all in a pile on the ground. We leaned against the F150 for the last time, and we watched for about one minute while a bulldozer ground our garbage into the ground, into that dusty barren ground where nothing would grow anymore. Then we climbed back into the truck and Yukon took me to the hospital, and by the time I was done at the hospital there was nothing left of the camp.

That's how it's supposed to be. The bush camp dissolves. The trailers go and the tents go and the vehicles go, and then the people float apart. The people camouflage again, disappear each of them, back into the wilderness of civilization.

The camp is designed to drift apart. Once the tents and trailers are gone — once the trees are gone — we aren't locked together anymore.

So then what?

Go and become a person again. Go back to your home, if you have one. Go back to your family and friends. Have a shower, lie in bed, and for god's sake, stop talking about it. You've talked about it long enough.

That's what they say: We get it, alright? We get it, already. You planted trees. Big deal. Move on.

96

My gallium scan, Day 72, was conducted by the same technician who did the bone scan —

The same one who'd watched me fall asleep on the hard-plastic scanning bed on Day 64, watched me jerk fearfully out of a dream — and that time, he'd kindly strapped my legs in place so that they wouldn't move, and he'd told me smiling that I could go back to sleep now.

So this time we talked. He was from the east coast. I'd planted trees there; we had a pleasant talk about it, for a while.

At the end I asked him:

So now what? How long before I get the results? Do I have to stay here?

He told me: Look — I'm not legally allowed to say anything — I'm not a doctor — So don't listen to anything I say — Technically I can't —

And he looked at the results of the scan, and said, There's no reason for you to wait here.

Which meant that the scan wasn't showing anything. It wasn't an infection. I was free to leave.

Arron and I stuck together for a few more days. We drifted south together, bummed around and got drunk. We rode out the momentum, shared the blow of sudden aloneness, of sudden foreignness and strange disoccupation.

On our last night in Timmins we slept in a hotel, and I had a bed to myself — a whole bed for the first time in months. I rolled around on that bed all night, physically swathed in comfort for the first time, and mentally stunned into awakeness by the silence and stillness in that room. After a few hours I went to the window, a ground-floor window facing a brick wall over an asphalt lot, and I tried to yank it open, found it screwed shut. My heart skipped a beat — for a split-second, claustrophobic again.

I spent that night listening to the air conditioner and watching the brick wall across the lot grow pinkish with the sunrise. I wondered how anyone is able dress themselves in the morning without being able to feel the air outside. How do you know if it's going to rain, when you can't hear what the birds are singing?

I guess people use weather forecasts. Or they stay indoors. Or do both at once.

97

I went to four more medical appointments before receiving a diagnosis. I spent the rest of the summer wearing an air cast — doctor's orders, in case it was a fracture.

It was early September when I was told that I had a bone bruise.

A bone bruise is just an almost-fracture: it is a breakage of the fibers on the interior of the bone, and a leakage of fluid from inside. The symptoms of a bone bruise are swelling and severe pain that can last for months.

The treatment for a bone bruise is rest.

It was an unlikely coincidence, all of that. It was an unlikely thing to bruise the bone directly underneath the site of a healing compound fracture — then to have this new pain arise on top of the old soft-tissue disturbance and the bone spur and the residual tenderness of the break —

All in the exact location where the existing hardware and the bone callus made it almost impossible to diagnose — and where the titanium rod prevented the use of an MRI. And it was just a coincidence, too, that I'd never finished that original course of antibiotics.

All of that confusion: just a stroke of bad luck.

It was Day 39 when I re-injured the bone, and I worked on it for more than a month after that.

Come August, I let it rest. In the middle of October, I found that I could walk without feeling pain.

No harm done.

98

So, what then?

That was always the question. The summer blew itself out again. It came to an end in a gently jaded flurry of drifting and drinking and lying awake at night. As it always did. The nights were getting colder and longer and I looked around and took stock of what I had.

I had a university degree, for the first time ever. A good education. And still I had a reasonable sum of tree-money rattling my pockets. I had two good legs to walk on — and I could almost run again, by then.

I had, too, that reckless momentum. I had that revving urgency and that sensation of Nothing-To-Lose. And I had — I was pretty sure — all the luck in the world.

Before the winter came, I went south — further south. In Nicaragua I lived in a remote shantytown, a village of three hundred intermingled families on an undeveloped coast. For two months I stayed with a family of six who ate only rice for three meals a day unless one of their dogs caught an iguana. The children lassooed wandering horses to ride bareback and they used machetes quite deftly for all manner of things. No one in the village spoke any English whatsoever.

I contracted chikungunya from a mosquito bite, and meanwhile by total coincidence I found myself in the home of a French ex-patriot doctor and her lesbian lover, and they cured me with herbal remedies and sent me on my way.

I hitchhiked through Costa Rica — caught rides on motorcycles, in cargo trailers and pickup beds, in eighteen-wheelers, family vehicles, and in a school bus full of uniformed kids. I worked, digging trenches with a pickaxe and chopping logs on a farm. I injected injured birds with shots of painkillers and I had to bury one of them the following day.

I shared a bed with a palm-sized whip scorpion; I let a tarantula crawl up my arm. I had a violent spat with an untamed howler monkey, was savagely bitten three times and then worried that I'd killed him.

I got deeply and totally lost in the jungle on the side of a volcano with three complete strangers. I witnessed an exorcism by accident. I spent a good month surviving on dumpster food while living with a couple of alcoholics and a recovering meth addict. I raised a thousand dollars in twenty-four hours and used it to buy a horse.

I slept on a wide open beach, in the sand; I slept in a corrugated-tin-roof shanty, in a hammock; I slept in a three-story water tower, in a bed.

I watched a hundred flawless sunrises above the Pacific. I cooked calamari for rich strangers, and I traded architectural drawings for food and bed. I washed laundry using well-water and I climbed through a lot of barbed-wire fences. I learned to skin iguanas and milk goats and I learned to train fighting cocks. I learned how to ride an old motorbike pretty well.

I learned how to speak Spanish.

And also I wrote a book.

99

Which means — you understand:

That leaves me here.

Here — now —

With the snow beginning to melt across Canada's southernish landscapes, and the days beginning to draw themselves out in the north.

And it will begin to look familiar up there, soon enough. The melting snow will flood the black-swamp moats and the landscapes will reveal themselves in churning greys and frostings of sharp-toothed ice. From underneath the snow there will arise those perennial incarnations of hell frozen over.

I don't need to see those landscapes, anymore. I already know what they look like. I know what they feel like. I've had enough of numb-white fingertips and cramping muscles, creaking elbows, splitting shins.

There are other ways to earn money —
    There must be, right? There must be.

I think there are ways to be comfortable. I think there are ways to get by without getting rained on — without getting frozen, burnt, slimy-slick and completely fucked up all the time. I know there are people who get by without getting so dirty, so hungry, so tired — who get by without getting pushed past that point —
    It must be possible. It could be nice.

I keep thinking that — it could be nice. It could be a good idea to go somewhere and find some job. Find a way to pay rent and I could take a shower every night — every night for the rest of my life.
    And then maybe I wouldn't get hurt, and maybe I wouldn't get crazy and drunk and obscene.
    And it could be a good idea.
    It could be.

But then —
    Well.
    Well, you know how it is.
    There's comfort, sure. There's comfort, in the Real World. And maybe there's safety and certainty too —
    But then what about the freedom?

I mean, what about the freedom and the clarity of it? The speed and the challenge, the earth and the air and the wildness of everything out there? The intensity, the absurdity —

I mean, what if I don't want to stop moving?

And it doesn't make sense —
It doesn't make sense but what if I get homesick?
Homesick for that stinking stampede, and the noise of them all, and the way that a person can get swept away. The way that the world can shrink to the size of some clearing in the bush, and how after the sunset there can be nothing at all but the moonlight and stars,
The breeze in the trees and the generator grinding away like a lullaby,
The sound of tents zipping shut, just a few steps away — the sound of coughing and them rolling over in the night — the sound of them there, just a few steps away —

I mean, do you know about that crowd?
Do you know that it can be warmer to wake up on the ground among that crowd — warmer and softer, more comfortable even — than it is to wake up in a bed?

So maybe you know and maybe you don't, but I guess it's pretty simple, what I'm trying to say.
I've made plans, and they're like this:
I'm going to buy a shin pad,
And then I'm going back to the bush.

About the Author

Kristel Derkowski was born in Newmarket, Ontario, and spent four years studying architecture at Carleton University in Ottawa. She also spent four seasons working as a tree planter in three different Canadian provinces between 2012 and 2015. The first draft of *Six Million Trees* was written while travelling in Nicaragua and Costa Rica, the final draft while living in a tent on the Fraser River and attending trade school in Hope, British Columbia. She is a certified welder apprentice who is also pursuing opportunities as a freelance illustrator and designer. She doesn't rule out going back to the bush — again.

Made in the USA
Middletown, DE
30 March 2016